SONAR

Insider

by Craig Anderton

SCHIRMER
TRADE
BOOKS

New York / London / Paris / Sydney / Tokyo / Berlin / Copenhagen / Madrid

Schirmer Trade Books
A Division of Music Sales Corporation, New York

Exclusive Distributors:
Music Sales Corporation
257 Park Avenue South, New York, NY 10010 USA
Music Sales Limited
8/9 Frth Street, London W1D 3JB England
Music Sales Pty. Limited
120 Rothschild Street, Rosebery, Sydney, NSW 2018, Australia

Order No. SCH 10153
International Standard Book Number: 0-8256-7314-3

Printed in the United States of America
By Vicks Lithography and Printing Corporation

Library of Congress Cataloging-in-Publication Data
Anderton, Craig.
 The Sonar insider : turbocharge your Sonar experience! / by Craig Anderton.
    p. cm.
  ISBN 0-8256-7314-3 (pbk. : alk. paper)
  1. Sonar. 2. Sequencer (Music software) 3. Music—Computer programs. I. Title.
ML74.4.S66A56 2004
786.7'4—dc22
                          2004009100

CONTENTS

AUTHOR'S PREFACE

Welcome to this book on getting the most out of Sonar. I've been using the program since before it was released to the public (one of the benefits of being a beta tester), and put it to work on everything from conventional songs to movie soundtracks. In the process, Sonar has shown itself to be an extremely versatile, intelligently-designed program with not just a superb feature set, but also an amazingly efficient workflow.

But a program with this level of depth can't be fully understood, let alone mastered, overnight. The manual can certainly handle the basics, and the online help is a great reference when you're in the middle of a project and can't quite remember that one specific trick or menu function. Still, there's a lot of potential lying just below the surface...and this book is designed to unlock that potential.

I've tried to avoid simply rewriting the manual; instead, this book spotlights some little-known features and procedures that can make your use of Sonar more pleasurable and speed you along the route to music production. In those cases where subjects covered here are in the manual, the emphasis is on talking about practical usages and applications.

This book has revised or adapted quite a bit of material from the Sonar Notes column I've been writing for *Sound on Sound,* England's premiere magazine for technologically-minded musicians. There's also some material from the Wizoo/Music Sales book *Sonar: Mixing and Mastering,* which is more a book about mixing and mastering that just happens to use Sonar as a platform. Both are useful sources for additional Sonar information.

Okay, that's enough for now: Boot up your computer, and start reading! I hope *The Sonar Insider* helps you realize your fullest musical and creative potential.

Craig Anderton

Douglas Spotted Eagle

Just about when Sonar 1.0 was released, I was asked to create some music for the Olympic Torch. I had less than three days to complete a fairly complex composition that represented the various cultures of the State of Utah. Even though I'd been using Cakewalk 9 and all the previous versions of Cakewalk since version 2.0, I was a little nervous, as I was on the road and didn't have much MIDI gear with me. Sonar and access to soft synths came to the rescue. I was able to use Acidized loops, Akai samples via an early version of V-Sampler, SoundFonts via LiveSynth Pro, and do it all on my laptop with a USB keyboard. I was psyched! The song was on every major network within 36 hours after I'd been asked to compose it. I never could have accomplished that task without Sonar.

I've grown musically with Cakewalk over the years, and they've been a huge part of my musical career as a recording artist for Windham Hill/BMG and Higher Octave/Virgin Records. After composing with just about every PC and Mac-based MIDI/audio product available, I've been extremely happy since building the new Sundance Media Group Studio A and B around Sonar, Mackie control surfaces, and various soft synths.

That said, add the expertise of Craig Anderton, a music industry legend, to the power of Sonar and the sum is this book. No one person has brought so much knowledge to the digital recording and music industry as Craig. Sonar can be an incredibly deep application with any number of workflows available, and many tools that casual users never encounter. Craig brings those workflows, tips, tricks, and techniques to all Sonar users on all levels. This book has so many gems to be gleaned, you'll come out knowing so much more that your productive and creative talents will be taken to a higher level. Mine certainly were, and I thought I knew Sonar inside and out. Reading through Craig's manuscript, I constantly found myself doing the mental head slap and saying "Dang, I didn't realize it could be done that way…"

Technology is a musician's best friend and worst enemy, as it can allow inspiration to flow easily, yet can also become a brick wall when the workflow is intimidating. Within these pages, Craig de-mystifies some of the hidden functionality of Sonar, and helps the reader to become not only more proficient, but more inspired. Owning this book is the next best thing to having Craig's phone number on speed-dial. Read it, re-read it, and then thumb through it in the quiet moments. Your music, your creativity, and your musical signature will be better for it.

Happy composing.
SPOT

(Douglas Spotted Eagle is a multiple Emmy and Grammy nominee, and co-recipient of the 2001 Native American Grammy for his production work on The Gathering of Nations *project. Douglas' Native Restoration Studios, with Tom Bee, has been largely responsible for bringing Native American music into the digital age; along the way, Douglas has fashioned a unique modern ethnic sound with his recently released* Voices *on Higher Octave Music and Nino Reyos' new* CD Warrior of Time, *which was recorded 100% in Sonar.*

Douglas has recorded 13 previous albums under his own name, and eight of those albums have achieved top-24 status on the Billboard charts. He collaborated with Peter Buffett on the Kevin Costner production of 500 Nations, *and Robbie Robertson on the score for* The Native Americans. *He has also scored or has been a featured in the scores of popular film/TV productions such as* The Truman Show, Thunderheart, Millennium, The Scarlet Letter, The X-Files, City Slickers, The Way West, Johnny Quest, Freaky Friday, The Last Samurai, Open Range, *and* Hidalgo.

Douglas is actively involved in film and new media production. He most recently produced Toubat, *an 80-minute documentary on the Native American Flute that was scored using Sonar, and has garnered several film festival awards.)*

Chapter 1

NAVIGATION AND USER INTERFACE

Sonar's user interface is highly customizable, and there are many tricks and shortcuts that simplify the navigation process. The more you master these techniques, the more you'll improve on Sonar's already excellent workflow.

TERMS OF ENGAGEMENT

Before proceeding, let's make sure we agree on terms for what we call various parts of the Sonar interface. Note that the term "Track View" usually means the combination of the Inspector and Tracks, Clips, and Bus Panes, as opposed to the Console View.

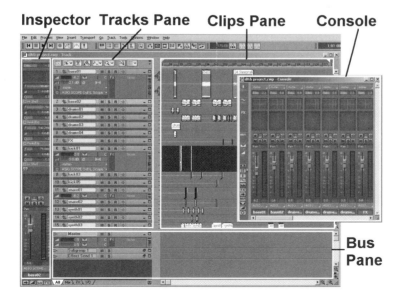

Here are the names for the main parts of the Sonar interface.

CLIPS PANE VIEW OPTIONS

To set the default view for MIDI and Audio Clips when you double-click on them:

1. Right-click anywhere in the Clips Pane.
2. Select "View Options."
3. Choose the desired view for MIDI Clips and Audio Clips.

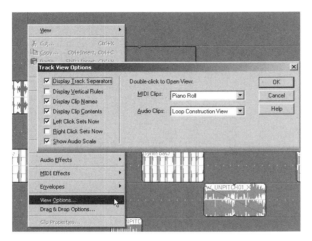

Right-click on the Clips Pane and select "View Options" to further customize the Sonar workspace.

Note the other check boxes along the left:

- **Display Track Separators** draws a horizontal line between tracks in the Clips Pane.
- **Display Vertical Rules** draws a vertical rule at measure lines in the Clips Pane. If you're zoomed way out, this makes the Clips Pane look rather cluttered; but when you zoom in, the rulers help you find your way around more easily.
- **Display Clip Names** and **Display Clip** Contents aren't really necessary if you're just using the Console View, but leave these checked so it's easier to identify the Clips.
- **Left Click Sets Now** and **Right Click Sets Now** determines whether one, or both, click types set the Now Time. I recommend checking Left Click and unchecking Right Click. There are many times when you need to right-click in the Clips Pane, and you don't necessarily want to reset the Now Time when you do.
- **Show Audio Scale,** when unchecked, butts the left side of the Clips Pane up against the right edge of the Tracks Pane. This gives a little more space for Clips, but then you can't click on the Audio Scale and

drag up or down to change the audio waveform scaling (described later). I advise checking this.

TRACKS PANE VIEW OPTIONS

Like the Clips Pane, the Tracks Pane offers several View Options as well. You'll find the "View Options" button (a downward-pointing arrow) in the toolbar above the Track Pane, just to the right of the Zoom Tool (magnifying glass icon). This button brings up several view customization features that influence how you interact with Sonar's interface.

You can make wholesale changes to the track view with just a few mouse clicks.

- **Show and Fit Selection** expands whatever Clips are selected (both horizontally and vertically) so they fill the screen. With a single track selected, this is like having a sample editor where you can see the waveform in great detail. All non-selected tracks are hidden.
- **Fit Tracks to Window** adjusts the height of all tracks so they fit within the current Track Pane size (within reason, of course...if you've recorded 65 tracks and the Track Pane height is a couple of inches, you'll see only the first few tracks).
- **Fit Project to Window** adjusts the project duration so that you can see the entire project, from beginning to end, in the Clips Pane.
- **Show Only Selected Tracks** hides all non-selected tracks. It's basically like Show and Fit Selection, except instead of being based on what Clips are selected, it's based on which Tracks are selected in the Track Pane.
- **Hide Selected Tracks** removes any selected tracks from view.
- **Show All Tracks** shows any tracks that were hidden.
- **Track Manager** brings up a window that lets you check and uncheck boxes to show/hide tracks (there's more on this later).

- **Show/Hide Inspector** provides control over whether or not you can see the Inspector.
- **Undo View Change** is exceptionally useful, especially because all you have to do is type "U." Want to zoom in on a waveform? Fine, but after doing any business with it, you'll likely want to return to the previous view. Just hit "U" and you're there. Similarly, "Redo View Change" (type "Shift+U") toggles back to the previous view.
- **Vertical FX Bins,** when unchecked, places FX bins horizontally as another field rather than as a vertical box.

AUDIO SCALING

Audio scaling changes the scale of a track's level display, without changing the track height. To change the scale, click and drag vertically along a track's left edge, where the calibrations are. Dragging up zooms in, dragging down zooms out.

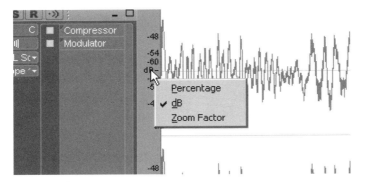

This shows a vocal track at the highest vertical audio resolution, which displays signal levels below about -42 dB. The signal is a combination of preamp hiss and mic handling noise. Incidentally, at normal resolution, this looks almost like a straight line. Keyboard shortcuts let you change resolution on all tracks simultaneously, or you can adjust individual tracks.

This feature is helpful when you want to cut audio exactly on zero crossings, check for DC offset, or make sure that loop endings fade out properly. It's also handy for gauging the noise floor. Right-click on the ruler to the immediate left of the waveform to choose its calibrations as dB, Percentage of full scale, or Zoom Factor (magnification amount). Double-click on the ruler to restore the view to minimum (default) resolution.

You can also change the resolution of all tracks simultaneously. This is important when splitting multiple tracks, as it's worth checking whether the split will cut the middle of any signal that might cause a pop or click. Use "Alt+Up Arrow" to zoom in, and "Alt+Down Arrow" to zoom out. (You can also Ctrl—

click on the standard track height vertical zoom buttons to change scaling, but keyboard equivalents are generally faster.)

RESIZING MULTIPLE TRACK HEIGHTS SIMULTANEOUSLY

If you've used Sonar for any length of time, you've doubtlessly come to appreciate the way you can change the Track height in the Tracks Pane to reveal fewer or more parameters, which also changes the height of the digital audio waveform display. But adjusting each track to show exactly what you want (*e.g.*, volume, pan, trim, and meters) can be a tedious process. That's why the following shortcut is so helpful, as it can cause any selection of tracks, or all tracks, to take on the same height as any *individual* track you adjust.

Here's the process:

1. Select the tracks that should follow your "template" track. If you want them all to follow, go *Edit > Select > All* (or use the key equivalent "Ctrl+A"). To select or de-select tracks, Shift-click on the track number (Ctrl-click does the same thing if you're more used to that key combo).
2. Press and hold the "Shift" key, then adjust the divider bar at the bottom of any of the selected tracks to set the track height.
3. After adjusting the track height, release the mouse button. Now all tracks are the same height, and display the same parameters. (Note: You could also press and hold "Shift" *after* adjusting the track, as long as you haven't released the mouse button yet. Adjust as desired, then release the mouse button while the shift key is being held.)
4 If you change your mind, just release the "Shift" key before the mouse button.

Incidentally, note that this doesn't work with the minimize/maximize buttons or any controls, just the track height. In other words, you can't select all tracks, hold Shift, minimize one track, then have all the other tracks minimize when you release the mouse button.

DOCKING TOOLBARS

You can dock toolbars at the bottom of the screen, not just the top. For example, it can be useful to segregate toolbars into two groups, according to the way you use them. You can also "float" toolbars anywhere in the program's workspace. Double-click on a docked toolbar's left "handle" to float it, and double-click on a floated toolbar's left edge to re-dock it.

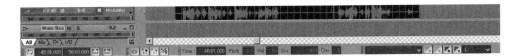

The Loop, Automation, Event Inspector, and Marker toolbars have been docked at the bottom of the Sonar workspace instead of the top.

TRACK SELECTION VS. TRACK FOCUS

When you click on a track's number in the Tracks Pane, the number's background turns blue (assuming you're using the default color scheme). When you click elsewhere on a track, it turns tan. So what's the difference between these two, anyway?

Blue means a track is selected for the purposes of performing some sort of operation, whereas tan means that track has the current focus. For example, if you want to mix down a selection of tracks to a mixed track, the tracks all have to be selected, as indicated by the blue background. If a track has the focus but is not selected, then it will not be included in the bounce.

Similarly, if you want to delete multiple tracks, select the ones you want to delete, right-click on one of them, select "Delete Track," and the selected ones will disappear. If a track has the focus but is not selected, it will not be deleted. However, if you right-click on the track that has the focus and delete it, not only will that track be deleted, but any selected ones will be deleted as well.

Here's a use for focus if you're into MIDI recording: Go *Options > Global >* "General" tab and check "Allow MIDI Recording without an Armed Track." Now, you can record into the track with the focus without having to arm it first—just click on "Record," and go.

THE NOW LINE "BUG"

I regularly see posts in Cakewalk-related forums along the lines of "When I try to place the Now Time right on the beat, it's offset by a small amount even with Snap off...and I can't place the Now Time where I want! The people who designed this program clearly have the mental capacity of a slug!" This is definitely someone who hasn't checked out the "fine print" in the Snap to Grid option.

• Navigation and User Interface •

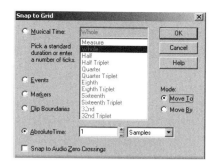

There's a lot more to Snap to Grid than just specifying a rhythmic value. Even with "Snap" turned off, "Snap to Audio Zero Crossings" remains in effect if checked. Here, "Snap to Zero Crossings" has been turned off, and the snap value set to zero samples, to give the maximum possible Now Time resolution.

If the "Snap to Grid" option is turned off, and if "Snap to Audio Zero Crossings" is checked, the Now line will still snap to zero crossings. This makes sense, because even if you don't want to snap to particular rhythmic values, you will probably want snap to zero crossings if, for example, you're looking for a splice point within an audio Clip.

For the finest Now line resolution, uncheck "Snap to Audio Zero Crossings," check "Absolute Time" as the snap option, enter 0 samples in the numeric field, and enable "Snap to Grid." This lets you place the cursor between samples. However, this is of limited usefulness—after all, why go for a resolution finer than what the program can offer?—so you may want to specify 1 sample as the Absolute Time value. That way, whether Snap to Grid is on or off, the Now Time will snap to the nearest sample.

And yes, I'll grant you that it's not necessarily intuitive that enabling Snap to Grid with a snap value of 0 samples can give finer resolution than disabling Snap to Grid!

GROUPS AND EDITING GROUP PROPERTIES

All the automatable parameters (including ones that are switched, such as Mute, as opposed to being continuous) can be *grouped* so that editing one of the parameters affects other parameters in the group. There are 24 groups, each indicated by a letter A-X, each of which has an associated color. Grouping is simple: Right-click on the parameter to be grouped, then select the desired group letter. Upon selection, the group's color occupies a thin strip at the left of the grouped control. Ungrouping works similarly. Just right-click on the parameter to be ungrouped, and select "Ungroup."

Even better, you can group dissimilar parameters (*e.g.,* pan and volume), and a Group Properties window provides considerable control over the relationship of control movements within the group.

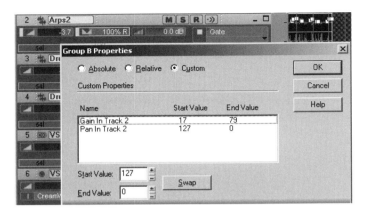

The Group Properties window determines how controls move in relationship to one another. Here, panning and volume track each other; however, panning covers the full range, while volume has limits of 17 and 79. If you use the pan control as the main automation control, the volume won't go lower than 17 or higher than 79. Using volume as the main automation control allows varying over the full range of the volume control, but the pan will hit its maximum and minimium values when the level is at 17 or 79 respectively.

Right-click on a grouped parameter and select "Group Properties." A corresponding window appears, where you have three choices concerning control movements:

Absolute—All controls move the same amount at the same rate. If one control hits a maximum or minimum limit before another control in the group, the other control can continue until it hits a limit too.

Relative—This works ratiometrically. For example, suppose two volume faders are offset by a certain amount. Reducing one control to half of its value reduces the other by half as well. Therefore, if several grouped controls have different offsets, they will all hit the -INF level at the same time during a fadeout because this mode preserves the *ratio* of any controls, not the *absolute* offset.

Custom—This sets up maximum and minimum limits for each grouped parameter. These can even reverse the "sense" of the control, so that as one control increases, the other decreases (useful for crossfading between two tracks with duplicate material but different processing, or if you want panning to follow volume in a particular way). Creating settings is intuitive: Click on the parameter you want to edit, then enter the maximum and minimum values.

As a practical example, suppose you've grouped several different drum tracks so you can bring the whole kit up and down with a single fader. You could set a lower limit for the kick, so that fading out would fade out all the drums up to a certain point; past that point, the other drums could still be faded, but the kick would always be present to keep the groove going.

But as they say in the late-night, paid commercial TV programs: "But wait! There's more!" If you find that entering numeric start and end values is too tedious, no problem: Set a fader to its desired start point, right-click on it, and select "Set Start = Current." Then set the end point, right-click again, and select "Set End = Current."

Furthermore, you can override a control's grouped status by holding down the "Ctrl" key while you move the control. And finally, you don't necessarily have to create a custom group to have custom settings; you can right-click on a fader in an Absolute or Relative group, then use the "Set Start = Current" or "Set End = Current" command.

THE MASTER BUS FADER

Some users have complained that Sonar doesn't have a master volume control for buses. This would be important if you were working on something like a surround project, and wanted to mix tracks down through six individual buses for a 5.1 output signal. (Granted, Sonar currently doesn't have surround panners or other surround functions, but as a workaround you can clone tracks and use level and panning for the two tracks to place a signal more to the left, right, front, or back. You can also dedicate separate buses to bass and center outs, and feed them with sends from various tracks).

However, there is a way to change levels on all buses simultaneously: Group them into one of 24 groups, just as you would group channel faders. The easiest way is to right-click on the volume control of each bus you want to group, and select the desired group from the pop-up menu.

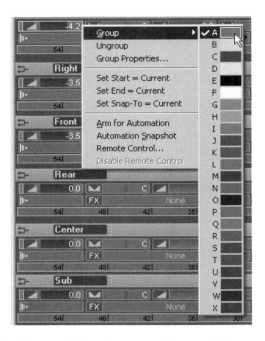

Just like channel controls, bus controls can be grouped into any of 24 groups. Groups are not separate for buses and channels—they draw from the same pool of groups.

But there's one other required step: Right-click on one of the grouped faders and select "Group Properties." In the Group Properties box, check "Relative" so that the faders work ratiometrically. That way even if the levels are offset, they can all go to the minimum level (-INF). You don't want to select "Absolute," as that preserves any offset; once the lowest-level fader hits -INF, the other faders can't be attenuated any further.

CUSTOMIZING COLORS

It's easy to make Sonar's Window backgrounds a little easier on the eyes during long sessions—white can be pretty glaring, and gray can be pretty boring.

You can see the colors change as you adjust them. For example, open a MIDI Piano Roll view. Then go *Options > Colors.* Under Screen Element, select Window Background, then check "Use Specific Color" rather than "Follow System Color." Click on "Choose Color," and use the standard Windows color picker to select the color of your choice.

While you're at it, here are some other screen elements you might want to modify. Don't go too nuts, because the default colors are fairly carefully chosen—for example, you don't want to choose a background color that's the

• *Navigation and User Interface* •

same as an envelope, thus obscuring the envelope. But the following are pretty safe:

Track View Control Outline. This determines the trim color around the various track parameters (*e.g.*, volume, pan, FX slot, etc.). I like to lighten the default color a bit so the control outlines stand out a bit more.

Track View Clips Pane Background. This is the gray background behind all the Clips in the Clips View. Making it a little bit darker allows the Clips to "pop" a little more.

Audio Clip Background. A very light robin's egg blue works well against the darker background.

Changing Wallpaper

For Wallpaper, check "Custom" to change Sonar's background from the default Sonar logo to something more pertinent, like your studio's logo (or picture of your significant other). When you click on "Custom," a browser opens up where you can select the desired BMP file; click on "Open" to apply it. Of the desktop images included with Windows, Soap Bubbles.bmp is kind of fun.

Changing Themes

If you want a completely different look, Sonar includes a variety of themes. To access these, go *Options > Colors,* then check the drop-down Presets menu.

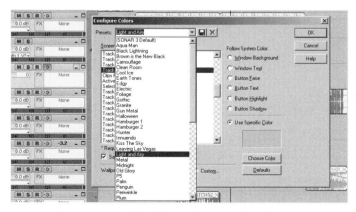

Not only can you customize the colors of individual elements of the Sonar interface, you can select any of several themes that produce radical interface changes.

You can create your own theme and save it by entering a name in the Preset field, then clicking on the "Save" button (floppy disk icon).

THE ART OF DRAG-AND-DROP CLIPS

Sonar supports a variety of drag-and-drop Clip options. For example, in addition to drag-and-drop within a project, you can drag and drop Clips among different projects that are open simultaneously. The rules are the same as for doing this within a single project: Dragging the file moves it from the origin to the destination. If you want to drag-copy the Clip, click on it, then hold the Ctrl key as you drag. Just remember to click on the Clip itself, not an any automation envelopes or fades that may be riding "on top" of it.

Note that if you've slip-edited the Clip (*e.g.,* shortened it), when you drag it, you drag the entire Clip. It still shows up at the destination as being slip-edited, but you can "unroll" the Clip to reveal the slip-edited part.

Sonar also has a "drag-and-save" option; see the chapter on Exporting Files for more details.

Traditional Drag-and-Drop Options

While we're in a drag-and-drop mood, let's look at some of the options Sonar allows when moving Clips around.

The drag and drop options are powerful, but double-check where you click, because what you select becomes the default—some users click on "Replace Old with New" and then wonder why moving a Clip deletes parts of older Clips. Until you find the default that works best for you (I use "Blend Old and New"), you have the option to check the box that says "Ask This Every Time" if you want to be asked each time to choose the appropriate action.

Right-click in any empty space in the Clips Pane, and choose "Drag & Drop Options." Under "What to do with existing material," you have several choices. "Blend Old and New" means that if a Clip overlaps another Clip, both Clips will play back during the overlap. If the "Automatic Crossfades" function is enabled, they will crossfade instead of mix.

"Replace Old with New" indicates that moving a Clip so it overlaps an existing Clip will delete the existing Clip in the overlapped range. If you check the "Delete Whole Measures" box, then the existing Clip will be deleted up to the beginning of the next measure that is not overlapped by the new Clip.

The main use for "Slide Over Old to Make Room" is when inserting a Clip at the junction of other Clips, or in the middle of a Clip. Everything to the right of the insert point moves further right to make room for the inserted Clip. If "Align to Measures" is checked, then the material slides over not just enough to make room for the inserted Clip, but until it hits the next available measure line.

Constraining Clip Vertical Movement

To constrain a Clip when moving it vertically in the Clips Pane, click on the Clip and hold down the mouse button. Then, hold down the "Shift" key while moving the Clip.

Moving Envelopes Along with Clips

Sometimes you want an envelope (volume, pan, etc.) to stay in place, but change the Clip affected by the envelope. Conversely, sometimes the envelope is an important part of the Clip, and if you move the Clip, you want the envelope to go with it. Sonar accommodates either option.

You can have envelopes migrate with Clips, or not.

nward arrow next to the cursor button. If "Select Track
:h Selected Clips" is checked, then any envelopes superimposed
move with it. If this is unchecked, the Clip moves independent-
lope.

FAST MARKER NAVIGATION

The main purpose for markers is to simplify navigation around a piece of
music, as you can jump to a particular marker without having to set the Now
Time or use the transport controls. It's important to strike a balance between
having too many markers, which can be confusing, and too few, which
makes it difficult to go exactly where you want. Markers can also identify
sections of a song, or lock to SMPTE time so they always indicate a certain
position in time, even if the song tempo changes.

The center for marker action is the Markers toolbar, so go *View > Toolbars*
and check "Markers." The toolbar can be floated or docked, but power users
will likely use key commands as often as possible rather than click on the
toolbar buttons.

If you hit "F11" on your QWERTY keyboard or click on the "Add Marker" button
while the transport is stopped, a dialog box appears where you can name
the marker, choose whether to lock it to SMPTE, adjust its placement, or assign
it a pitch to which Groove Clips will transpose automatically. You can call up
this dialog box for a previously-placed marker by right-clicking on the marker, regardless of whether or not the transport is playing.

To add markers in real time while the tune is playing, you again press "F11" or
click on the toolbar's "Add Marker" button (the marker symbol with the +
sign). Unlike dropping a marker while stopped, though, this won't let you
name it—you'll have to name it later (right-click on the marker symbol, then
type in the desired name).

You can also go *Insert > Marker,* or right-click on the ruler and select "Insert
Marker" (the marker goes at the current Now Time, not necessarily where
you clicked), or Ctrl-click on the space above the time ruler, where the markers hang out...but those seem like more effort. Markers are placed without
regard to the Snap grid, but if you move or copy them, they will snap to the
selected grid value.

So now the markers are placed...time for navigation! Drop markers at strate-
gic points in a song, then name them (Verse 1, Verse 2, etc.). You can jump

• Navigation and User Interface •

among markers in several ways, and all of these are functional while the tune is playing:

1. Click on the toolbar's "Next Marker" or "Previous Marker" button.
2. Use the menu—*Go > Previous Marker* or *Go > Next Marker*.
3. Use Sonar's key equivalents (Previous Marker = "Ctrl+Shift+Page Up," Next Marker = "Ctrl+Shift+Page Down").
4. Use the Key Bindings function (under the Options menu) to assign what I think are more logical equivalents: Previous Marker = "Shift+F11," Next Marker = "Shift+F12."
5. Select a Marker from the drop-down list toward the left of the markers toolbar.

If the Markers toolbar isn't enabled, you can still get to them easily. Hit "F5" twice, and you'll see a list not only of markers you've created, but also loop start and end, punch points, beginning, end, and the select (from/thru) points. Click on the appropriate marker, then hit the computer's "Return" key twice. The first "Return" places the marker's time in the *Go > Time* window. The second "Return" places the cursor at that time, which instantly becomes the Now Time. You can also jump to one of these markers; double-click on the desired Marker, then click on "OK" when the Go box appears. Of course, another option is to use the marker toolbar's buttons to jump to the previous marker or the next marker.

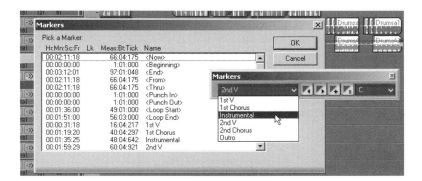

The Markers List is in the background, while the front window shows the Markers toolbar. Selecting a marker from the drop-down list toward the left of the toolbar jumps the Now Time to that point; the buttons (from left to right) are go to previous marker, go to next marker, add marker, and open Markers List.

To edit a marker (or markers) and then jump to a particular location, click on the Markers List view button (the one to the immediate left of the Project Pitch drop-down menu at the right of the Markers toolbar). This shows the same basic list as the markers drop-down menu, but you can delete markers, change marker properties (*e.g.,* change the name or Groove Clip pitch), insert a marker at the current now time, or lock a marker to SMPTE time so that changing tempo doesn't change the marker's location (useful when adding sound effects to video productions—the tempo of a tune may change, but the time in the film where the space ship blows up may not). After doing any desired editing, click on one of the marker entries, and the Now Time jumps to that marker.

It's also possible to print this list, which doesn't seem all that helpful for music, but would be great for documenting where sound effects fall in an audio-for-video project.

In addition to navigation, markers serve one other purpose: Clicking between any two markers in the strip just above the time line causes them to define a time range selection. You can of course also set this to a loop by clicking on the "Set Loop to Selection" button.

FLOATING WINDOWS

Normally, Sonar windows are bounded within Sonar's workspace. Moving them past that point cuts off the window at the workspace boundaries.

However, you can set any window to "float" mode, and move it over to a second monitor, even if Sonar's workspace is confined to one monitor. Click on the button in a window's upper left-most corner, and select "Enable Floating." To return to non-float mode, do the same thing but select "Disable Floating." Easy!

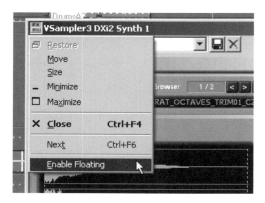

Any window can be made to float, this freeing it from the confines of Sonar's workspace and allowing it to be moved to a second monitor. In this case, VSampler3 is about to be floated so it can have its own space in the second monitor.

THE TRACK MANAGER

The chapter on Mastering tells how to have a single track take up the Clips Pane by selecting a track, then typing "H" when the focus is on the Track Pane. Another way to do this is to right-click on the track number (or any empty space in the title bar) and select "Show Selected Tracks." All other tracks will be hidden, and the selected track will take over the entire Clips Pane. Either options gives you a fine environment for audio editing.

If you want to move up a notch in flexibility, type "M" to check out the Track Manager, which lets you show/hide groups of tracks.

The Track Manager window has three toggle buttons for Audio, MIDI, or Buses. Clicking on one of these buttons toggles between selecting and deselecting the corresponding tracks. Hitting the Space Bar will check (track shown) or uncheck (track hidden) the selected tracks. A good application for this is to hide MIDI tracks for virtual synths during the mixing process. Presumably by that point all the MIDI data driving the synths is finalized, so you're interested solely in modifying the audio mix of the instruments. Hiding the MIDI tracks helps reduce clutter.

All the MIDI tracks driving virtual instruments have been selected, and unchecked so that they will be hidden when the Track Manager dialog box is closed.

Using the toggle buttons and Space Bar to make selections is a short cut. You can always check or uncheck whichever tracks you want; the changes take effect when you click "OK."

TRACK SORTING

When you've recorded a lot of tracks, it can be very convenient to sort them according to name, output, channel, size, etc., as well as do things like put all the archived or muted tracks at the beginning or end of the track list. This is a task for the Sort Tracks function.

Select all the tracks in the Track Pane (type "Ctrl-A" or go *Edit > Select > All*), then go *Track > Sort*. When the "Sort Tracks" box appears, check the criterion by which you want to sort, the order ("Descending" or "Ascending"), then click on "OK."

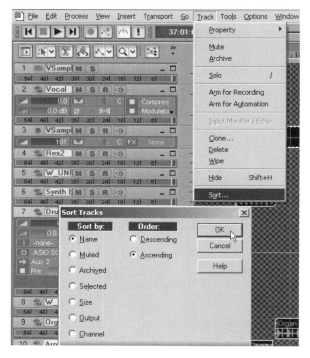

The selected tracks are about to be sorted by name, in ascending order.

FAST TRACK PROPERTY CHANGES

With Sonar's new busing structure, you may run into situations where you bring in an older project, and want to assign all the tracks to a new bus (for example, the project defaults to sending them all to an available hardware output, but you want to send them to a master bus which then feeds the hardware output).

It's easy to do mass bus reassignments. This technique is useful not just for re-assigning the track outputs to different buses, but for situations where you want to change any group of track output assignments (*e.g.,* drum and percussion outputs) to a particular bus.

Of course, you can always change each track output assignment individually. But there's a much faster way.

Select the tracks whose output assignments you want to change, then go *Track > Property > Outputs.* Select the desired output from the "Audio Outputs" drop-down menu, click on "OK," and all the tracks will feed the newly specified output.

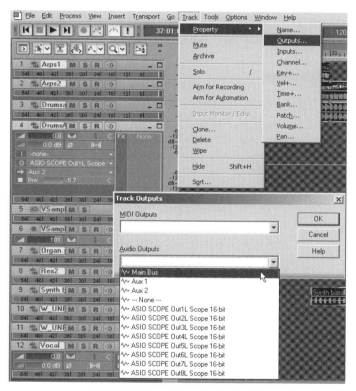

You can change common parameters (such as output, input, channel, etc.) for all selected tracks using the Track Properties options. In this example, all the audio tracks from an older Sonar project are about to be reassigned to a Main bus instead of a hardware output.

This same technique can also change other track name, input, level, and pan properties. It works with MIDI tracks too, where perhaps mass changes are even more useful, as you can change channel, key, velocity, patch, and other parameters for multiple tracks.

THE ZOOM TOOL

When you need to zoom in quickly on some detail of the Clips Pane, use the Zoom Tool. You can find this in two places: In the toolbar above the Tracks Pane (the icon looks like a magnifying glass), and to the right of the Clips Pane, just above the "Zoom Out" button.

To use the Zoom Tool, click on its button in either location, and the cursor turns into a magnifying glass. Draw a marquee around the area you want to zoom, and when you release the mouse button, the marquee will expand to fit the Clips view. At this point the cursor returns to normal. You can go back to the previous view by hitting "U."

If you want to do a series of zoom moves, instead of clicking on the Zoom Tool, hold down the "Z" key. As long as it's held down, the cursor will be a Zoom cursor. To revert to the standard cursor, release the "Z" key.

SCISSORS VS. SPLIT TOOL

At first I didn't see much use in the Tracks Pane toolbar's Scissors Tool, because you can always split a Clip by stopping, placing the cursor where desired, and hitting the "S" key. But the key word here is "stopping." With the scissors tool, you can split a Clip without having to stop. This is very handy when looping, as you can cut up and modify a loop or Clip in context with the music.

To call up the scissors tool while in the Clips Pane, type "C."

SIMULATED "FOLDER" TRACKS

The bus structure introduced in Sonar 3 allows a variety of sub-grouping options. One of these creates the rough equivalent of Cubase SX's folder tracks. The folder track is a great idea; you can dump all related tracks (*e.g.,* several outputs from a soft synth, along with the MIDI tracks that control it; or all the percussion parts used in a drum track) into a single folder, which neatens up your workspace.

In Sonar, suppose you want to put all your drums and percussion in a folder track. You can't, but you can create a "Drum Bus" that goes to either a main bus or output, and assign all the drum tracks to it. Now, Hide the drum tracks (and if appropriate, any associated MIDI tracks), then set the level of the entire kit—or add plug-ins to it—using the bus track. (Type "M" to call up the Track Manager, where you can uncheck those tracks you want hidden). You can have several of these premixes in the Bus Pane, thus freeing up Tracks Pane real estate.

For effects, multiple buses provide far more flexibility. For example, suppose you want several instruments to go through tempo-synched delay, but also want them to go through a reverb. Furthermore, you want other tracks to go through the reverb, but not the delay. You can create a delay bus, and assign that to a separate reverb bus; tracks that need reverb and no delay can have sends that go directly to the reverb bus.

LAYOUTS

The Layout function lets you add, name, or delete particular layouts of windows and pane sizes. I first found out how useful this could be while working on a project that involved extensive use of both MIDI and digital audio, which required switching back and forth a lot between the Piano Roll view and the main Track View. So, I set up layouts for the two views, which simplified switching between them.

Any time you want to save a particular layout, go *View > Layouts > Add*. This brings up a window where you can name the layout. After naming it, click on "OK," which adds the new layout to the list.

You probably don't want to add too many layouts, as scrolling through a long list of layouts to find the one you want is kind of annoying. But at least for me, I don't need too many. In addition to the layouts mentioned above for the piano roll and track views, I typically use three more:

Console view on top. I arrange the layout so the console's right edge extends slightly beyond the right-most side of the track view. That way, if the track view is on top, it's easy to click on the console's edge to bring it back to the front again.

Sample editing. This changes the Time Ruler Format to samples, and makes the Clips Pane section very wide compared to the Tracks Pane (when sample editing you usually don't need to access the aux send controls, ins and outs, etc.).

Track info. This is the usual track view, but with the Tracks Pane extended way to the right, with just a bit of audio showing. Calling up this layout provides the equivalent of a console view without having to use the console, as you can see auxes, pans, the complete track names, which effects are loaded in the fx bins, etc. In particular, this makes it easy to sort out the panning, as it's easy to tell if most tracks are centered, to the right, to the left, etc.

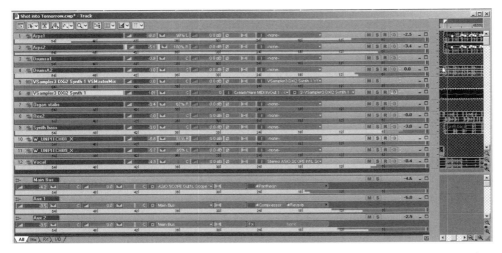

This layout is extremely useful when you want an overview of all of a tune's parameters. For each track you can see the name and number, track type, volume, pan, phase, stereo/mono, track input, status (mute, solo, record), and metering.

The Window Layouts function has a couple other notable options. If you check "Close Old Windows before Loading New Ones," open windows that are not a part of the new layout close before the new layout loads. I find this helps keep clutter to a minimum. I also check "When Opening a File, Load Its Layout." In addition to being able to save Global layouts, when you save a song with a particular window layout, this layout will be called up when you open the song. If this box isn't checked, then Sonar opens to the usual default track view.

Finally, to make the layout window as convenient as possible, try using the key bindings function to assign the layout window to function key F2. To do this, go *Options > Key Bindings,* make sure "Computer" is selected as the "Type of Keys," scroll down the "Key" list until you see "F2," then click on it. Next, scroll down the Function list until you see "View | Layouts." Click on it, then click on "Bind"; hitting "F2" will now call up the Window Layouts.

Once the window is open, you can use your computer keyboard's up/down arrow keys to select the desired layout, then hit "Return" to load—no mousing required!

• Navigation and User Interface •

THE POWER OF TEMPLATES

Templates are special files that Sonar identifies as default projects that you can choose when you create a new project. 47 templates are currently provided; some relate to specific kinds of recording situations, while others have default setups for specific pieces of gear, such as mixers or General MIDI modules. However, you can also make your own templates, save them, and recall them.

Sonar looks for folders in a specific location, as shown under *Options > Global > Folders > Templates* (you can change the default directory path here if so desired). If you save template files to this folder (the default path is C:\Program Files\Sonar 3 [Producer or Studio] Edition\Sample Content), they will appear in the list of available templates when you select "Create a New Project" upon opening the program.

To create and save a template, first set up the program exactly as you want—window positions, buses, MIDI and audio tracks, etc. Then go *File > Save As...* and under "Save as Type," select "Template." This adds the suffix .CWT to the file name.

If at some point you want to delete or rename templates, you can do so within Windows. Go *Options > Global* to see where Template files are stored (default is the "Sample Content" folder in Sonar's program folder); find the file, right-click on it, then select "Delete" to delete it or "Rename" to rename it.

METERING TWEAKS

Sonar has always let you change VU meter resolution, but now that there are meters for the hardware interface outputs, this function is more useful than ever. To change resolution for a meter (in any view), right-click on it and choose a range of 12, 24, 42, 60, 78, or 90 dB. Each meter can have its own range.

With the Console view, I generally set the output meters for 12 dB. This lets me monitor those all-important peaks, and gauge the approximate amount of loudness maximization that may be required. (For example, if the meters make it to 0 but otherwise spend very little time in those upper 12 dB, then the track will definitely need to be made "hotter" during the mastering process.) On the other hand, I set the input meters for maximum (90 dB) resolution so I can see if there's noise or crud at the lower range of an incoming signal.

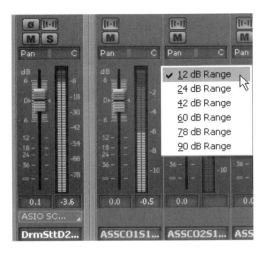

The channel meter on the left has a 90 dB range, while the output bus meter on the right has a 12 dB range. Note the calibrations running along the right side of each meter.

In Tracks Pane, you can also set the meters for vertical or horizontal configurations. To do this, go to "Meter Options" (the right-most button in the "toolbar" above the Tracks Pane) and select the desired option. When vertical, the meters become more like overload indicators, because when you collapse the track to a short height, you basically see only activity and clipping. If you prefer to use the Console or Inspector for mixing, this is a good choice; you can see more track parameters in the Tracks Pane, as the vertical meters don't take up space along the bottom.

If you generally mix using the Track View rather than the Console, then you can extend the width of the Track Pane, enable horizontal metering, set them to a fairly wide playback range, and enjoy high-resolution metering.

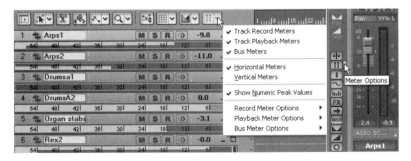

Horizontal meters have been chosen for Tracks Pane, and set to a resolution of 60 dB. The right section shows where to find the Meter Options menu in the Console View.

Also from the Tracks Pane Meter Options button, you can choose characteris-
... Record, Playback, and Bus meters. These include a choice of Peak,
... ...nse, whether playback meters are pre or post fader,
... ...er, post fader, or pre fader and post FX.
... equivalent meter settings for the

...k and Console views to be far more than
... of material. For example, the Console
... ...dicate average signal levels, while the
... which are more important when record-
... ...bably better set to post-fader, so you
... contributing the most amount of level.
... ...s lets you monitor track activity so you
... ...l, regardless of the fader position.

The end result is that the ... ...g options are just one more reason why I
tend to mix in Console view, but track and edit in Track View.

Just remember that meters do use up CPU power (albeit not much), so if you
really need that last ounce of performance, disable any meters you don't
need. From the Meter Options, you can enable or disable Track Record, Track
Playback, and Bus meters individually.

MAKING THE BIG TIME EVEN BIGGER

The Big Time feature (go *View > Big Time*), which shows the current measure
or SMPTE time in large type, is pretty useful if you need to see where you are
in a tune, but aren't right in front of the computer (*e.g.*, you're several feet
away, overdubbing your part with a guitar or keyboard).

You probably know that clicking in the Big Time window alternates the readout between Bars/beats/clocks and SMPTE time, but if you right-click in the
window, you'll be able to change the font, point size, style, and color (style
can't be changed, though). For maximum visibility, I recommend the Arial
Black font, yellow for the color, and 96 point size (the maximum size you can
use, but you'll have to type "96" in the Size field; the "preset" font sizes don't
go that high).

This is also very useful if you're working on audio-for-video projects with a dual-monitor setup: "float" the Big Time window over to your second screen, and you'll always be able to see exactly where you are at a glance.

Even singers in the vocal booth will be able to see where they're supposed to come in if they can see the monitor, and you make the Big Time display big enough. This shows the results of setting the type to Arial Black at 96 points.

2

MIDI

Although digital audio gets a lot of attention these days, MIDI is having a resurgence due to the rise of virtual instruments, which are driven by MIDI data. Sonar has unusually deep MIDI talents, so let's investigate.

MIDI PLUG-INS

There's a lot of excitement about plug-ins, whether audio processors or soft synths. But the humble MIDI plug-in (which Cakewalk calls MFX), long a fixture in Cakewalk products (and now supported in Cubase SX), also deserves some attention. Granted, it may not be quite as sexy to massage MIDI data as it is to warp audio beyond all recognition or play a dead-on accurate emulation of some impossible-to-find vintage synth, but MIDI plug-ins definitely have their uses.

MIDI plug-ins work very much like the audio kind. They can process a track or input signal in real time, or be applied destructively to anything from individual Clips to complete tracks. There are three ways to process MIDI data with a MIDI plug-in:

- In the Tracks Pane, right-click on a MIDI track's FX slot, and navigate to the desired plug-in.
- In Console view, right-click on the black FX slot just below the track name at the top, and navigate to the desired plug-in.
- Select the Clip(s) to be processed, then go *Process > MIDI Effects* and choose the desired plug-in.

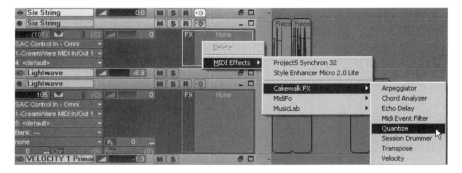

There are several ways to open a MIDI plug-in, but the easiest option when you're in the Tracks Pane is to right-click on a MIDI track's FX slot. This reveals a tree that can access all available MIDI plug-ins.

The first two options happen in real time: As you play the input device or track, the MIDI effect processes the data. To make this processing permanent, select the Clip(s) to be processed and go *Process > Apply MIDI Effects.*

The final option works somewhat differently. When the effect appears, it has an "Audition" button. Click on this to hear the effect applied to a portion of the data. If the piano roll view is open, Sonar will re-draw the data to show the effect of adding the plug-in (*e.g.,* if you're using the Echo Delay plug-in, you'll see the additional echoed notes). These changes are also visible in the Clips Pane.

When you click on "Stop," the Clip stops playing, and the data reverts to how it looked before. Click on "Cancel," and the selected data remains unchanged. Click on "OK" to apply the effect to the data permanently.

Applying MIDI effects is crucial if you save your file as a Standard MIDI File, because the MIDI effects are not part of the SMF spec. When you apply the effects to a track, upon saving the file the track's data reflects the results of any processing.

Cakewalk Plug-Ins

Sonar includes several MIDI plug-ins of varying usefulness; here's a brief rundown.

Chord Analyzer. This looks at MIDI input or track data every 1 to 128 MIDI ticks (you set the "sampling rate"), displays the notes being played on a keyboard, shows the notes on a staff, and tells you what chord it recognizes. If the chord is ambiguous (*e.g.,* the voicing is the same for an F major chord or A minor+5, 2nd inversion), the analyzer will display all voicings it recognizes.

This plug won't make a profound difference in the course of Western civilization, but it's a useful learning tool.

Echo Delay. You can specify delay in ticks, milliseconds, or rhythmic value (or tap tempo), the number of echoes, velocity decay rate from one echo to the next, whether echoes are transposed (chromatically or diatonically, up or down, and the interval), and swing value. Cut this baby loose on 50% swing, and you'll be impressed. Echo Delay makes it particularly easy to play those staccato, "dugga-dugga-dugga" synth parts that serve as rhythmic underpinnings to many dance tracks. The only downside is that long, languid echoes eat up synth voices.

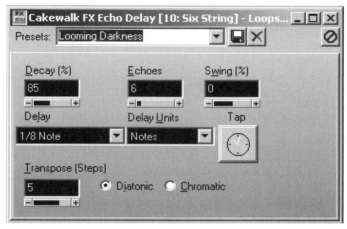

Swing adds interesting rhythmic effects to echoes, and can be a negative or positive amount. It is possible to set a decay percentage above 100%, in which case each successive echo becomes louder.

MIDI Event Filter. You may already be familiar with the *Edit > Select > By Filter* option, which applies editing only to specific types and/or values of events. The MIDI Event Filter is a quicker way to achieve some types of filtering, as you can easily create presets regarding which data to remove (*e.g.,* Channel Aftertouch or Key Aftertouch), as well as specific value ranges (such as all Key Aftertouch events with values under 10, or all notes with durations under 5 ticks). I find the way to get the most out of this plug-in is to create presets that take care of common editing situations, like removing unintended aftertouch data.

Arpeggiator. This is the one I should like the best, but it has a couple problems. Although it works fine with real time input, it does not operate properly on data within a track. Furthermore, if you apply it, it does create arpeggiation—but each note has only a single tick's duration, so you generally need to quantize the length to a particular rhythmic value using *Process > Quantize*. As a result, this is a fairly cumbersome plug-in to use, albeit one with potential if there's a fix in its future.

Quantize. Doesn't Sonar already have a quantize function? Yes, but remember the plug-in works in real time. I find this indispensable for doing quick quantization on, say, a drum part while laying down tracks—the part remains unaltered, so I can take off the plug-in later and do any permanent quantizing with a bit more finesse. This plug-in has what you'd expect from a quantization plug-in: resolution, strength, swing, window, offset, randomization, etc.

Transpose. This flexible plug-in has capabilities that far exceed just going through the usual *Process > Transpose* route. It will transpose by intervals or diatonically, but can also transpose from one key to another, and change scales in the process (as well as show which notes are mapped to which target notes). It's also possible to create a custom transposition map (which can also serve as a drum mapper if you're not into using Sonar's drum grid view), and constrain notes to a particular scale if they fall outside the "accepted" roster of notes for a given scale.

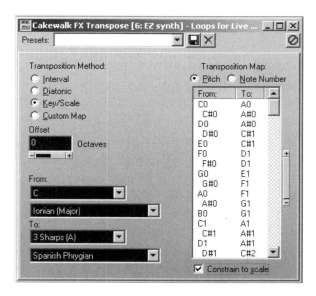

Here material recorded in the key of C, based on the Ionian scale, is about to be transposed to the key of A and constrained to a Spanish Phrygian scale. The note map toward the right shows the original notes and the target notes to which they are mapped.

Velocity. This offers several tricks you can't do with *Process > Scale Velocity*, such as set all velocities to a constant, add or subtract a constant, scale to a certain percentage of the current value, randomize, and limit range (*i.e.,* velocities lower than a certain limit are brought up to that value, whilst velocities higher than another limit are reduced to that value). This function is well-suited to "compressing" the amplitude of MIDI data; scale everything by 50%, then add 64 to all data for approximately 2:1 data compression.

Session Drummer. Need a quick rhythm track? This plug-in is so useful it has its own section...coming up next!

The Sonar Drum Machine

Session Drummer makes it easy to put together a temporary drum track, which can be way more interesting than the average metronome. We'll assume you're starting a tune from scratch, and want to assemble a drum pattern as rapidly as possible; following is one way of how to do this.

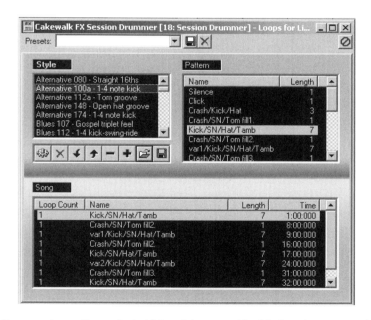

Session Drummer is a pattern-oriented "virtual drum machine" designed to put together quick drum parts for practicing, or as an improvement over the boring click-click-click of a metronome. You assemble songs a pattern at a time; each pattern can repeat for the number of times you specify.

First, open a new project. When the New Project File box appears, choose the "Session Drummer" template, then click on "OK." The Session Drummer window appears, along with a Project having a single MIDI track. If you plan to drive an outboard MIDI drum box, you're set up.

But let's use an internal DXi synth, like the Edirol VSC. Go *Insert > DXi Synth > Edirol VSC;* when the "Options" screen appears, make sure that "MIDI Source Track," "First Synth Output (Audio)," and "Synth Property Page" are checked. In the corresponding MIDI track that appears, assign the "Ch" parameter to "10: VSC GM2 Rhythm" (you will likely need to extend the bottom of the MIDI track to see this parameter).

If there are any drum patterns in Session Drummer's lower pane, click on the delete (X) button on the Session Drummer toolbar (below the Style pane) to start with a clean slate. Then, choose the desired Style from the Style pane; the Pattern pane presents related pattern options.

To audition a Pattern, click on it, then click on the Transport Play button. To use the Pattern in your tune, double-click on it; the Pattern shows up in the lower Playlist pane. To change the number of Pattern repeats, double-click on the Loop Count parameter, then enter the desired number of repeats.

Keep adding Patterns to the playlist. To delete an individual Pattern from the list, click on it and use the keyboard's Delete key or the Session Drummer toolbar's (-) button. The same toolbar has up and down arrow buttons to move a selected pattern up or down in the list. You can audition the part you've constructed at any time, but note that it always starts from the tune's beginning.

When you've finished the drum part, you can convert it to track data. Close the Session Drummer window, and make the MIDI Drum Track the active track (click on its Tracks Pane track number). Go *Process > MIDI Effects > Cakewalk FX > Session Drummer*. The Session Drummer window reappears with whatever Patterns you programmed. Click on "OK," and the Session Drummer deposits data into the selected MIDI track. Click on play, and you'll hear your part.

The Synchron 32 MIDI Plug-In

Cakewalk's Project5 includes a MIDI plug-in step sequencer called Synchron 32. Although you can use this within Sonar, it takes a bit more work because functions that are "in the background" with Project5 need to be done manually within Sonar.

Basically, each Synchron 32 pattern can be triggered by a corresponding MIDI note. If you right-click on the Note Listing toward the left, you can specify the lowest trigger note. For example, if you choose C0, then pattern A1 plays when Synchron 32 receives C0, pattern A2 plays with C#0, pattern A3 plays with D0, and so on.

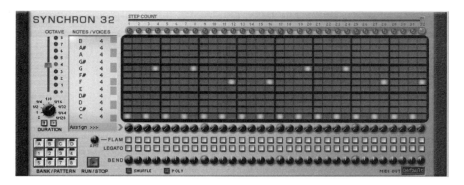

Project5's Synchron32 step sequencer can be used in Sonar to create MIDI patterns.

Enter the note corresponding to the pattern you want to play in the MIDI track being processed by Synchron 32, and extend the note for however long you want the pattern to play (Synchron 32 won't latch to a note). Note that you can trigger multiple patterns at the same time by entering several notes. This makes it possible to build up complex, polyphonic step sequences out of several monophonic sequences.

MidiFo Plug-Ins

A quick trip to the web will reveal several manufacturers of MIDI plug-ins for Sonar (and frequently, also for Cubase SX). One company, MidiFo (**www.midifo.com**), has released several plug-ins including a MIDI LFO, Step Sequencer, and four plug-ins designed to process Continuous Controller signals (Quantize, Random, Thin, and Velocity).

The Step Sequencer has much in common with Synchron 32. Patterns are mapped to notes, and like Synchron 32, you need to enter a note within the track being processed by the step sequencer to play the pattern. It offers up to 64 steps, with independent control over note value, gate, and velocity value, and up to four controller values per note. Additional parameters control swing, step length, and loop type (forward, reverse, random, etc.). It's also possible to play just a portion of the sequence by entering a start and end step, and because you can map each of 128 patterns to various notes, playing multiple notes plays multiple patterns simultaneously.

The MIDI LFO is a novel and useful plug-in that generates waveforms including sine, square, random, sawtooth, various harmonic sines, etc.; you can also select a step sequence to create more of a sample-and-hold type effect from the controlling waveform. Of course, all of this is tempo-synched. The output can be continuous controllers, NRPN values, pitch bend, aftertouch, or even sys ex (although you better get out your pocket protector for this one—you need to know your bits and bytes).

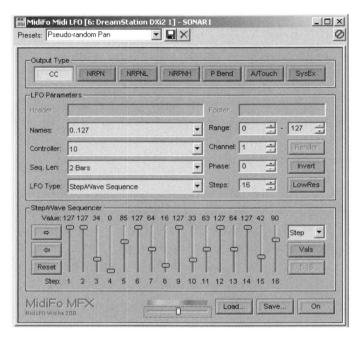

The MIDI LFO is set up to produce a panning effect by generating controller #10 messages, as determined by the LFO's step sequencer waveform. In this example, the panning pattern repeats every two measures.

One of the presets gives an idea of this plug-in's versatility: An oscillator drift function that adds random pitch changes. I use the MIDI LFO to generate periodic controller waveforms (these get written to the track when you apply the effect). I've always liked the feature in Cubase SX where you can "draw" tempo-synched control curves based on particular waveforms; the MIDI LFO takes this concept further, although admittedly, it also takes more work to get where you're going.

The Continuous Controller processors are more utilitarian, but nonetheless have their uses. Thin CC does what you'd expect—thin out a controller to minimize the potential for MIDI choke, with filtering done on the basis of time (*i.e.,* how close together the messages are) as well as value. Quantize CC is a bit different, though. It quantizes the values of a continuous controller to one of several possible values. For example, if you quantize volume into four steps (the maximum possible is seven), then anything falling within volume values of 0-32 would be set to 32, values within 33-64 would output at 64, etc. Actually this isn't always the case as there are highest and lowest value scaling sliders, but you get the idea. Obviously the output will sound "stepped" with low quantizing values, but in some ways, that's the point.

Velocity CC outputs the specified controller whenever it receives a note on, but with its value scaled by the note-on's velocity. This makes it easy to tie particular controller values to velocity so that playing hard produces more of some particular effect. Random CC produces a random value of a particular controller when triggered by either a note-on or note-off command.

THE VIRTUAL MIDI GUITAR

Compared to keyboards, one of the great aspects of guitar is those wide-open voicings that use a mix of open and fretted strings. If you're a guitar player who dabbles at keyboards, odds are you can play the basic majors, minors, and so forth. But what about those wonderful jazz voicings that you're only comfortable with when playing guitar? And what if you're a keyboard player who knows a little guitar, but has a hard time fingering some of the more challenging guitar chord shapes?

MIDI guitar is a possible, although pricey, solution. Fortunately, Sonar has a workaround for getting guitar voicings in a keyboard world.

Start by loading a suitable patch, guitar or otherwise, from a soft synth or external tone module. Decide which MIDI track will contain the notes, make it the active track, then go *View > Staff* (keyboard shortcut: "Alt+7"). Then click on the guitar neck button (located between the "Next Step" and "Tab" buttons) to show a guitar neck with 21 frets.

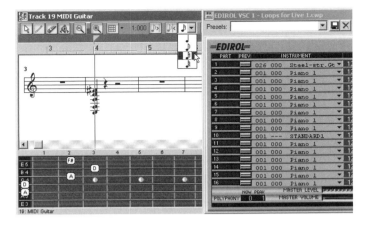

Sonar makes it easy to step-enter guitar chords. Here, a guitar D chord (with 5th as the root) is playing back through a guitar patch on channel 1 from Sonar's Edirol VSC soft synth. The pop-up menu is being used to select a 16th-note display resolution, and in a tribute to all the Telecaster fans reading this column, the maple neck option is selected. Note that only a portion of the neck is visible; it's being covered up by the Edirol VSC.

Right-click on the fingerboard to choose from rosewood, ebony, or maple fingerboards, in high or low graphic resolution (no, you can't choose between a Les Paul or Strat scale length). As entering data here is a step-entry process, there's a pop-up menu so you can choose the desired note duration.

Click on the measure indicator above the staff where you want to enter the chord. Then click on the desired notes on the fingerboard, or on an open string (*i.e.,* below the first fret). Like a real guitar, you're allowed one note per string. As you enter each note, it will show up as notation on the staff. As with any other kind of notation screen entry, you can cut, copy, paste, etc. individual notes or groups of notes.

Notes within a region show up as blue; if you start playback, notes will light in red as they sound. Otherwise, notes are black. You can play the next note/chord or previous note/chord by clicking on the Play Next or Play Previous buttons (the ones with the shoes, as in "step"); it's also possible to show Tablature.

Now for the *pièce de résistance:* Open the Piano Roll view, and edit the chord notes to create a strum effect. To do this, "spread" the note attacks so that the lowest note starts a bit ahead of the beat, the highest note starts a bit behind the beat, and the other note attacks follow an even gradient between the highest and lowest notes. You can also try spreading the chord so that the highest note hits right on the beat. This provides a different kind of phrasing; guitarists use both, depending on the feel of the song.

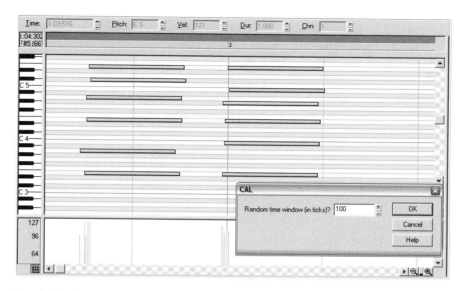

If you're in a hurry to get a strum effect, go Process > Run CAL > Random Time.cal. *Specify around 100 ticks of variance. This isn't as good as adjusting notes individually, but at least prevents simultaneous attacks, which sound very unlike guitar. Note how the attacks for the two chords are staggered.*

Offsetting the notes will make the notation screen look less pretty (what is the notational symbol for "a few MIDI clocks ahead or behind the beat," anyway?), but the sound will be much more realistic.

SECRETS OF THE PIANO ROLL

Features with a lot of power can be confusing if not fully understood—like the way Cakewalk lets you see as many or as few MIDI tracks as you want, simultaneously, within a single Piano Roll view. Actually, this is one of the reasons I use Sonar—MIDI remains a big part of what I do, and I like this sort of "big MIDI workspace" approach.

The piano roll view is nothing really new: it has the usual piano keys for pitch reference, grid to line up notes, and a controller strip along the bottom for viewing velocity, pitch bend, modulation, etc. The unusual aspect is the Track Pane strip toward the left, which lists each selected track and has selection boxes for Show/Hide Track and Enable/Disable Editing. Additional buttons let you enable Solo, Mute, and Record from within the piano roll view.

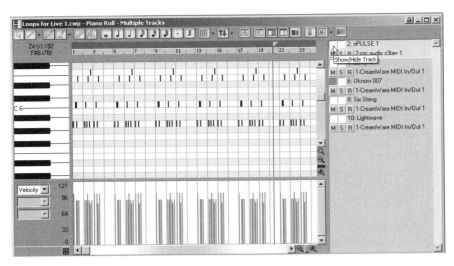

The Piano Roll view can show multiple tracks simultaneously; the Track Pane strip toward the right side lets you choose which tracks to show or hide, and which will be affected by editing operations. Additional buttons provide shortcuts for showing all tracks, hiding all tracks, and inverting tracks (i.e., showing ones that are hidden, and hiding ones that are showing).

To see multiple tracks, select them in the Tracks Pane (i.e., Ctrl-click on the Track numbers you want to select) and go *View > Piano Roll* or type "Alt-5." If you double-click on a single Clip (and Piano Roll is selected in Track View Options as the default result of double-clicking), then only that Clip will appear in the piano roll view, and any other selected tracks will be de-selected.

If multiple tracks are selected, now you can choose which tracks to work on and view. Click on a colored Show/Hide box to hide a track's notes and controllers, click on the same box when white to view the track again. The box to the right of Show/Hide controls whether editing operations are enabled on not. When gray, editing operations will not affect the associated track; when white, they will.

I find this feature particularly handy with drum parts, as despite having a dedicated drum editing view, in some situations (like developing loop library "construction kits"), I still prefer to record each drum on its own MIDI track. Being able to see as many or as few as I want in the piano roll view is great: For example, I can see the kick, snare, and high-hat simultaneously, but quantize only the kick, or lag only the snare...or quantize pairs of tracks. It's also convenient to be able to see kick and bass at the same time, left and right hands of a split keyboard part, or particular combinations of guitar strings with a MIDI guitar part.

There are a few fine points involving this screen. The scrubbing function (which if you haven't discovered yet is well worth checking out) works only with tracks that are both shown and enabled for editing. If you disable a track *or* hide it, it will not be scrubbed.

Also, note that there's a difference between the active track with the focus (the background of the Tracks Pane track name is tan) and a selected track (the background of the Tracks Pane track number is blue). When showing multiple tracks in the piano roll view, if you hide the active track no editing is possible.

There are also four useful shortcut button. The seventh button from the right (with the arrow that points left) shows/hides the piano roll's Track Pane. The button to its right shows all tracks, and the next button to the right hides all tracks. Continuing to the right, "Invert Tracks" hides all tracks that are shown and shows all tracks that are hidden. This is useful when you're alternating your edits between two groups of tracks, *e.g.,* kick/snare/hats and high/mid/low toms.

Another shortcut is that you can select all notes of a particular pitch in the Piano Roll view by clicking on the corresponding keyboard key toward the left of the window.

BOUNCING CLIPS

To consolidate multiple Clips of MIDI data in a track into a single Clip, select the Clips, right-click on any of these Clips, then select "Bounce to Clip(s)." To do this for all Clips in all tracks, choose "Select All" (or type "Ctrl+A"), then do the bounce.

Chapter 3

LOOPS AND LOOP RECORDINGS

One of Sonar's strongest features is the ability to do on-the-fly time stretching/compression. This lets digital audio loops run at different tempos than their original recording, or follow along with tempo changes. However, tweaking loops for optimum performance can take some effort.

Sonar uses the principle of dividing an audio loop into rhythmic "slices," each of which represents a discrete sound, a sound group (*e.g.*, kick drum and snare hitting at the same time), or rhythmic interval, such as a 16th note. When you change a loop's tempo, each slice's start point shifts to accommodate the change. For example, if the original loop is at 130 BPM and there are slices every 16th note, if you change tempo to 140 BPM, the slice start points will move closer together to retain a 16th note relationship.

Speeding up generally truncates or time-compresses the decay, because the ear is most interested in where the attacks fall. Slowing down extends the decays to lengthen the slice accordingly. Note that slice timings are adjusted by DSP-based "stretching" processes; another stretching method, found in REX format files (described later), physically cuts digital audio into pieces and plays these back with MIDI notes.

PERFECTING GROOVE CLIPS

The key to successful time-stretching with rhythmic loops is making sure the slices fall exactly at attack transients. There must also be enough slices to define the beat, but not so many that the loop gets cut up excessively, thus creating sonic artifacts or other glitches during the stretching process.

Sonar can read "Acidized" files, which have pitch and tempo information embedded in them according to Acid's file format. These are already sliced (whether they're optimally sliced or not is another issue), and will follow tempo (and pitch) changes. However, a non-Acidized file (Sonar accepts WAV, AIF, and MP3) will not have these time-stretching properties until you convert it into what Sonar calls a Groove Clip. This automatically adds slicing markers, which you can edit later to optimize the stretching process.

After importing the audio into the Clips Pane (either via *File > Import Audio,* or simply dragging the file into the pane from the desktop or possibly another program), right-click on the Clip and select "Groove-Clip Loop," or use the "Ctrl-L" keyboard equivalent. In the Clips Pane, a Groove Clip acquires rounded corners instead of the square ones associated with regular audio Clips. You can convert multiple Clips to Groove Clips by selecting as many as desired, then typing "Ctrl-L."

Tweaking Groove Clip Sliders

When you play back a Groove Clip, if it's standard, percussive-oriented material without swing, odds are Sonar will make a decent guess about where the slices need to go, and you'll be able to change its tempo without having to tweak. But not all Clips are so accommodating, especially when slowing down tempo. Editing markers is usually mandatory for drum loops played by human drummers instead of machines, as editing can compensate for any timing variations that interfere with the stretching process.

However, even parts generated by drum machines with metronomic precision may need some tweaking. For example, suppose a Clip has a lot of swing applied to a 16th note hi-hat pattern. Sonar can place slices every 16th note, but the "swung" notes don't fall on that particular rhythmic grid.

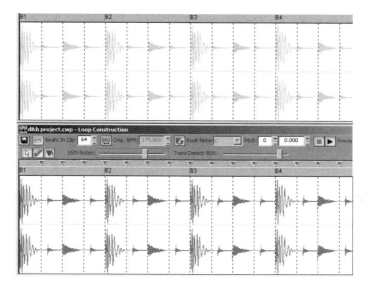

These two Clips in the Loop Construction window have slices every 16th note. The top one has no swing, and all the drum sounds line up with the 16th note grid. The lower Clip has significant swing, and while the kick (the big blob of audio located at B1, B2, B3, and B4) and the open hi-hat (halfway between each kick) line up perfectly, the swung, closed hi-hat sounds do not.

Slowing down a loop where slices don't line up with attacks produces "flamming" due to the difference between when the program thinks the hi-hat *should* hit, as opposed to when it actually *does* hit. Speeding up the loop may not sound as bad, because the flamming gets closer together. In fact, all programs that use slice-based time-stretching work most efficiently when speeding up rather than slowing down. Therefore, if you want to create a loop that works well from, for example, 100 BPM to 120 BPM, you're better off creating it at 100 BPM and speeding it up than starting at 120 BPM and slowing it down.

In any event, if stretching a loop degrades its sound quality, some tweaking will almost always make it sound better. The place to edit slices is the Loop Construction view, which you reach by double-clicking on a Groove Clip (assuming Loop Construction has been set as the default view, as described in the chapter on Navigation). It has two main slice editing sliders: A Basic Slices slider that determines the rhythmic interval between slices, and a Transient Detect slider. The higher the Transient Detect percentage, the smaller the transient Sonar will consider a percussive attack.

In general, use the longest rhythmic values and lowest transient detection possible, consistent with the loop stretching properly. For most dance-oriented drum loops, 8th- or 16th-note slices with a transient setting of 0%–20%

---

works well. In fact, before getting too much into editing, try adjusting the Basic Slices and Transient Detection sliders first. Often choosing different values will solve flamming and other problems, without the need for editing.

Editing Groove Clip Slice Markers

Loops that don't stretch properly require editing the slice markers. Each marker has a small, triangular-shaped handle. Editing involves lining up markers with attacks to teach Sonar the loop's precise rhythm. Optimally, you want the marker to line up at the precise beginning of the transient; zoom way in to get this as close as possible.

Once you move a marker by selecting it and dragging it (you can type "S" as a short cut for calling up the select tool), its triangle turns blue to show that it has been edited. You can also insert markers anywhere by double-clicking where you want the marker, on the same horizontal line as the other triangles. Because inserted markers are not generated automatically, they too will have blue handles.

Sonar will endeavor to keep any markers that you've moved manually in their assigned positions, so you can experiment at any time with the Slicing and Transient Detect controls without losing the positions of your carefully-placed markers.

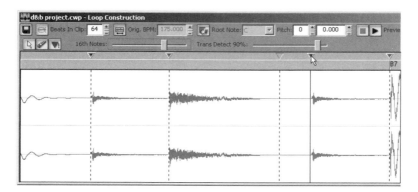

A marker has just been dragged from its old position (indicated by the triangle's "hollow" look) to the attack of the swung hi-hat just before beat 7. Upon releasing the mouse to complete the drag operation, the old marker's outline goes away. Note the blue handle in the modified marker.

Note that high Basic Slice and Transient Detection values may add unneeded slices where no attacks exist, which also require editing. These degrade the sound by splitting sustained sounds or cutting off drum decays (this is particularly annoying with kicks, as you lose some of the fullness and "ring"). To remove a slice marker, click on the eraser tool (or type "E" to call it up), then click on a marker's handle to delete it.

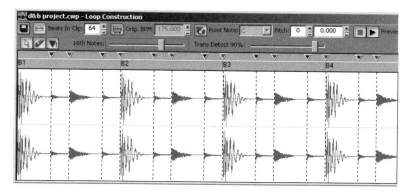

This tweaked Groove Clip has several of the original markers moved from their original positions to match up with the swung hi-hat notes.

All this editing may sound like a lot of work, but it's more complex to explain than it is to actually jump in and move markers around to match up with attacks. Your reward for doing so will be Clips that can change tempo without flamming or artifacts, assuming you're not trying to stretch too terribly far.

THE MULTITRACK LOOP EXPLORER

The Loop Explorer window's main function is to audition loops, which you can then import into the program and convert into Groove Clips. But you can also audition multiple loops simultaneously in this window. This is particularly useful with "construction kit" sample CDs that might have several loops for snare, hi-hat, percussion, and so on; you can test the parts together to see how well they work. Similarly, you could check out how a bass loop sounds with a particular drum loop.

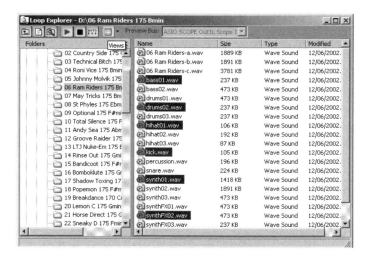

Several loops have been selected in the Loop Explorer window. Clicking on the Play button plays them all at once; if Auto is enabled, additional loops play as soon as they're selected.

Unless the loops are "Acidized" Groove Clip loops, you're limited to loops of the same tempo if you want them to all play together in rhythmic sync. Also, you can't include loops from more than one folder. Nonetheless, multitrack loop exploration is still a very useful technique. Here's how to do it.

1. Click on the first loop to select it.
2. Click on the Loop Explorer's "Play" button.
3. To add a loop, Ctrl-click on another loop in the Loop Explorer's list of files.
4. To de-select an already-selected loop, Ctrl-click on it again.

I prefer to enable the Loop Explorer's "Auto-Preview" button, as whenever you select a loop, you'll hear it play with the others. If "Auto-Preview" is off, then you need to hit the "Play" button every time you select a new loop in order to hear it.

This works best for loops stored on your hard drive. Loops auditioned from CD-ROMs are okay too, but because they have slower data throughput than a hard drive, the audio engine may stop when you add another loop, necessitating a quick click on the Play button.

Finally, after selecting all the loops you want to use, you can drag them over en masse to the Track Pane.

HAVING CLIPS FOLLOW PITCH

In addition to following tempo changes, a Groove Clip can also follow pitch transposition information embedded in a tune. However, to make full use of this feature, it helps to understand the interplay between the Project Pitch, Groove Clip reference note, and Pitch Offset parameters. Here's an overview of how the process works.

Establish the Project Pitch

This provides a baseline reference of the song's key against which transpositions are referenced. (Note that this is not the same process as setting the key signature and meter, which affects the Staff view for notation.) To do this:

1. Go *View > Toolbars*.
2. Check the Markers toolbar so that it's visible.
3. Set the Project Pitch from the drop-down menu in the Marker Toolbar's right-most field.

Define a Groove Clip's Pitch Parameters

You can access the four parameters that relate to following pitch from the Loop Construction window (double-click on the Groove Clip to invoke), or for a more compact version, from the Clip Properties windows (right-click on the Groove Clip, then select the "Groove-Clips" tab).

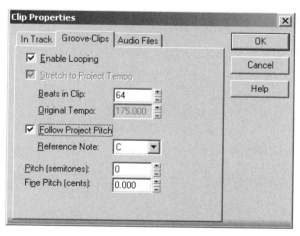

Parameters that determine whether (and how) a Groove Clip follows pitch are accessible from the Loop Construction window, or from the Clip Properties window shown here (accessed by right-clicking on a Groove Clip).

The four parameters are:

- **Follow Project Pitch.** Check this if you want the Groove Clip to follow pitch changes embedded in the project. Note that for drum parts, you will likely want to leave this unchecked, unless you prefer the drums' timbre to change when the Project Pitch changes (which can work well sometimes as a special effect).

- **Reference Note.** Set this to the Groove Clip's original recorded key (*e.g.*, if it was originally recorded in the key of E, select E from the drop-down menu). Better-documented sample CDs usually include the key information for samples.

- **Pitch (semitones).** This offsets the Groove Clip's pitch in semitones (up to ±2 octaves), regardless of whether or not "Follow Project Pitch" is enabled. For example, suppose the Groove Clip was recorded in G, the Project Pitch is G, "Follow Project Pitch" is enabled, and you set the pitch parameter to +1. The Groove Clip will now play back at G♯. If the Project Pitch changes to C, the Groove Clip will now play back at C♯. If "Follow Project Pitch" is not enabled, the Groove Clip will always play back at G♯ (an offset caused by setting the pitch parameter to +1 compared to the original Groove Clip pitch).

- **Fine Pitch (cents).** This offsets the Groove Clip's pitch in cents (up to ±50 cents), and works exactly like the Pitch Offset. This is an *invaluable* feature for loops that are slightly out of tune.

Insert Pitch Changes Into the Tune

Now that we have Clips that can respond to pitch changes, let's insert some pitch change markers so the Clips know when to change. Click on the Time Ruler at the top of the Clips Pane where you want the pitch change to occur, then hit "F11" (or right-click where you want the change and specify "Insert Marker" from the pop-up menu).

When the Marker window shows up, go to the Groove Clip Pitch drop-down list and select the new pitch reference. Name the marker if desired. Click on "OK," and you're done.

Incidentally, if you expect to cut up a Groove Clip into smaller Clips, set the "Follow Pitch" parameters before you cut, so that all the segments retain the data you programmed. If you cut up the loop *before* setting these parameters, you'll have to enter them for every Clip derived from the loop.

ADDING FADES AT LOOP BEGINNINGS AND ENDS

When a loop repeats, the splice needs to be seamless. This requires that the start and end levels be identical. (It's a misconception that these *have* to be at 0; they can be any level that's equal. However, matching levels to 0 is easiest). The simplest way to insure this is to add a very quick fade-in and fade-out to the Clip. The optimum time seems to be about 2-4 ms, or around 80 to 100 samples at 44.1 kHz.

After drawing the fade-in and -out, loop and play the Clip to make sure there aren't any clicks or pops. Some loops may need a little more of a fade, or the concave instead of convex fade curve (right-click on the fade curve, and choose the desired shape).

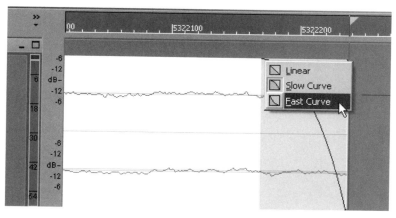

Zoom way in, and use the fade tool to draw the appropriate fade. The fade area will be shaded, making it easy to see where the end falls along the Time Ruler (here the fade is about 70 samples). Note that right-clicking on the fade curve has opened a pop-up menu, where you can choose the fade curve. In this example, Fast Curve is about to be chosen.

To save this fade with the click, click on the Clip to select it, and go *Edit > Bounce to Clip(s)*. You end up with the same Clip in the same place, but this time, with any fades you added. Drag it off Sonar to the desktop, and the saved Clip includes the fades.

ELIMINATING GROOVE CLIP DISTORTION

After working with Groove Clips for a while, I noticed a strange problem where even though the Clips were normalized to something less than 0 (e.g., -0.1 dB), the track meters sometimes indicated overload. As I couldn't figure out a solution myself, I asked the Cakewalk engineers if perhaps the meters showed clipping at a value slightly less than 0, but Cakewalk confirmed that the meter clip point is 0. Hmmm...

After putting in a lot of editing hours on my next loop library, I finally figured out what's going on. If a file plays back without distortion, is converted into a Groove Clip, and plays back at its "native" tempo, it will not distort. However, speeding up or slowing down the song may cause slight volume increases that push the overall level past the point of overload. This is because the DSP that does the time-stretching relies a lot on crossfading, so if phase-coherent audio sections overlap, the signal peaks could add up and exceed the available headroom.

This effect is not predictable. For example, a 120 BPM Groove Clip might distort at 80 and 140 BPM, but not 160 BPM. So, when creating Acidized files, my final step is now normalizing them to -3 dB.

Unfortunately, Sonar does not allow normalizing to anything other than full code (0 dB). You might think that normalizing within Sonar, then going *Process > Audio > 3 dB Quieter,* would accomplish the same result as normalizing to -3 dB. For some reason, though, that's not the case.

So, I use Adobe Audition (formerly called Cool Edit Pro) to call up the file, then go *Effects > Amplitude > Normalize,* check the "Decibels Format" box, check "Normalize to" and enter "-3 dB," leave "DC Bias Adjust" unchecked, then click on "OK." So far, I have yet to create a Groove Clip that will distort, regardless of tempo, when normalized to -3 dB although of course, anything is possible.

There is one other detail: If you click on a Groove Clip within Sonar and select Adobe Audition from Sonar's Tools menu, Sonar will not let you go there because it assumes that wave editors can't handle Groove Clips. Therefore, I just open up Audition, call up the loop file(s), and normalize to -3 dB...done.

A FINE POINT ABOUT PROCESSING GROOVE CLIPS

Sometimes when you apply an audio process within Sonar to a Groove Clip, it loses its grooviness and reverts back to regular audio...and sometimes it retains its acidizing markers. Here's why.

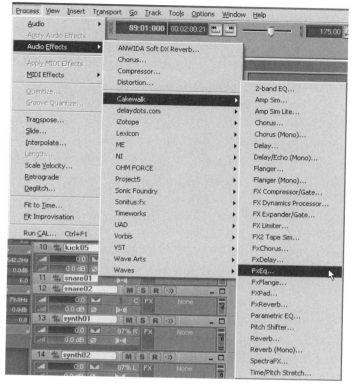

Using the Process > Audio Effects *path to select effects allows Groove Clips to retain the markers that enable time-stretching, even after processing. Here, the Cakewalk FxEq is about to be selected.*

If you reach the effect by using the *Process > Audio Effects* path, choose the effect, and click on "OK" to apply the effect, the file being processed will retain the Groove Clip acidizing markers. This has worked with the Cakewalk effects I've tried, as well as those from other manufacturers. However, if you insert an effect in the FX slot and go *Process > Apply Audio Effects,* the Groove Clip reverts to a standard type. If you work a lot with Groove Clips, it's a good idea to get into the habit of using the *Process > Audio Effects* function.

There is a catch: Auditioning the effect is more of an off-line process. First, the Transport needs to be stopped. Then, calling up the effect presents you with an Audition button (this won't be present if the sequence is playing when you call up the effect). Make your edits, hit "Audition," and wait for Sonar to build a temp file. Don't like the results? Hit "Stop," edit some more, audition, and wait. When it sounds the way you like, hit "OK."

Fortunately, there's a faster workaround. Insert the effect in the FX slot, edit in real-time to your heart's content, and when everything is just as you like, save the settings as a preset. Then go *Process > Audio Effects,* call up the effect and preset, then click on "OK." Just don't forget to remove the effect from the FX slot when you're done, otherwise you'll hear the effect applied twice—once from the processing, and once from the real time FX slot effect.

RETROGRADE GROOVE CLIPS

This tip, from Cakewalk's Carl Jacobson, is for groove and beat fans. Its object is to reverse the order of the slices within a Groove Clip, thus creating a new variation on the loop. This works best with loops that are staccato, and have sharp attacks. Otherwise, when continuous sounds are broken up, clicks can occur at the splice points.

Start off with an Acidized WAV file, or Clip that has been converted into a Groove Clip using Sonar's Loop Construction window. Select the file, then go *Process > Audio > Reverse.*

Next, disable Groove Clip looping for the file (click on it and type "Ctrl-L," or right-click and deselect "Groove-Clip Looping"). Once the file has been con-verted into a standard audio Clip, again go *Process > Audio > Reverse.*

Finally, re-enable Groove Clip Looping. Press "Play," and enjoy the retrograde fruits of your labor.

A DERANGED TIMBRE-SHIFTING APPLICATION

The Groove Clip function is one of my favorite Sonar features. But it's not just a way to loop, it's also a way to process rhythmic tracks in totally bizarre ways. Try out these effects, you won't believe your ears...

1. Double-click on a loop to bring up the Loop Construction window.
2. Set the "Pitch" parameter to +24.
3. Set "Trans Detect" to 100%.
4. Press "Play" or "Preview" to start the loop playing.
5. Experiment with the "Slicing" slider. Start with 64th notes for the most robotic/metallic effect, then try 32nd, 16th, 8th, etc. Each slice setting produces a different type of freakazoid effect.

These bizarro loops seem most effective when layered with the original loop, which should be set to normal loop settings. They also make great break-beats when you drop out the original loop.

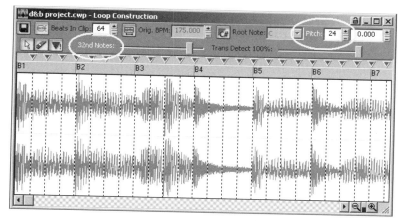

Forcing the Loop Construction window to "incorrect" parameter values can produce some great robotic/synthetic timbres. The key is to set pitch to 12 or 24, and a high "Slices" value (in this case, 32nd notes; both parameters are circled in yellow for clarity).

Although +24 is a somewhat "magic" pitch parameter, +12 also produces useful effects. -12 and -24 give weirdly pitched, slowed-down effects that also sound fabulous layered with the original loop. Often, you can simplify the loop beats by setting the "Trans Detect "slider to a low value, like 10%.

Bottom line: want some really weird, but musically useable, loops? The Loop Construction window is a gold mine of possibilities—just learn how to tweak the "wrong" settings.

SLICING WITH SONAR

There are ways to time-stretch other than "Acidizing" files. Propellerhead Software's ReCycle is a wonderful program that allows high-fidelity time-stretching for drum loops, as well as some other loop types. It does this not with digital signal processing algorithms, but by taking a piece of audio and cutting it into physical, separate slices—not just the "virtual slices" indicated by markers in a waveform.

"Sliced," tempo-stretchable stereo files created with ReCycle have a .RX2 suffix and are called REX files. Although the end result is similar to Groove Clips or Acidized files—the sound can stretch to different tempos—there are times when stretching a file via slicing can sound better than DSP-based time-stretching.

For best results, each slice should have a single, discrete sound or group of sounds (*e.g.,* kick, snare+kick, bass note, spoken word, hi-hat, etc.). These are then triggered via MIDI, so that if (for example) a particular slice falls on measure 1, beat 3, it will be triggered at that point regardless of tempo. Therefore, tempo changes don't affect the sound quality, just the triggering time of a section of the original piece of digital audio.

As of this writing, Sonar doesn't support REX files directly. Until it does, here's a workaround.

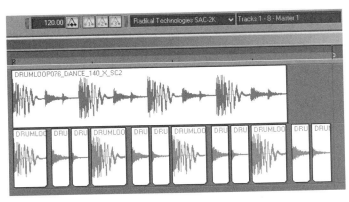

The upper track is the original 140 BPM, 1-measure drum loop. The lower track has been "sliced" at each drum transient, and the tempo changed to 120 BPM (as shown in the upper left). Note how the interval between triggering successive slices is longer, which reflects the fact that the tempo is much slower. As a result, each slice doesn't last as long from a rhythmic standpoint as at the faster tempo. Nor does the original loop equal one measure any more, because it's still a 140 BPM loop.

1. Import the loop you want to slice into a Sonar audio track.
2. Set Sonar's tempo to the same tempo as the loop.
3. Zoom in on the waveform to be sliced so you can easily identify where the various attacks fall.
4. Turn off quantization.
5. Select the scissors tool, and use it to cut at the very beginning of every significant transient (you can also click at the point you want to cut, and type "S").

That's all there is to it. Now when you change tempos, the slices will trigger at different points to accommodate the change.

Here are a few tips regarding this technique:

- When speeding up the tempo, the decay of the previous slice will spill over into the next slice's attack. Generally, this won't be a problem. If it is, just shorten the duration of any slice that spills over into the next slice's attack.

- With slower tempos, gaps will open up between the slices. If the gaps are too abrupt, add a slight fadeout toward the end of the slices. (ReCycle extends a sound to fill up any gaps.)

- Processing individual slices can lead to wonderful kinds of mayhem, not unlike some of the fun you can do with Cyclone DXi.

CROSSFADE LOOPS FOR PADS

Suppose you have a great sustained synth pad, like a drone or held note (or even a guitar power chord), and you want to turn it into a loop. However, unless the loop start and end points share the same level and timbre, the process of looping will impart a rhythmic quality due to the change in sound when the loop repeats. Of course, this diminishes the pad effect.

Fortunately, we can borrow a solution from the sampling world called *crossfade looping,* as long as there's some audio in the original sample prior to the loop start point. Note that for best results, the part you want to loop should not be normalized; there should be at least a few dB of headroom, because what we're about to do may increase the signal level by a dB or two in a few places.

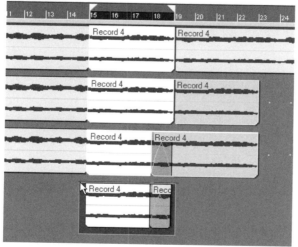

This diagram shows the process of creating a crossfade loop in a step-by-step style. The top strip shows the original audio, and how a four-bar loop has been isolated through splitting. The next strip down shows that the audio to the right of the original Clip has been deleted, and the original Clip has been copied and dragged to the right so that its end point and start point meet. In the next to last strip, the beginning of the copy crossfades over the end of the original Clip. Finally, after removing the excess audio to the right and left of the part to be looped, select the original Clip and crossfaded section so that the two pieces can be bounced into a single Clip.

To begin, convert the section you want to loop into its own Clip by adding a split at the start and end (place the Now Time over the start and type "S" on the keyboard, then do the same for the end). Next, delete any audio to the right of this newly-created Clip.

Drag-copy the copied Clip to the right so that its beginning butts up against the end of the original Clip. Now slip-edit the beginning of the copied Clip toward the left, which creates a crossfade with the end of the original Clip. As a result, upon reaching the end of the loop, the original Clip will include some of the audio leading up to its beginning—the secret of creating a perfect splice.

Now all you need to do is split once more on the crossfaded section's right boundary, so that the crossfaded section is on top of the original loop. Draw a marquee around the combination of these two Clips to select them, then go *Edit > Bounce to Clip(s)*. The crossfaded section will mix in with the original Clip. If you loop this Clip, it should transition seamlessly from end to beginning.

All that's left is to turn it into a Groove Clip (the quickest way to do this is to select the Clip, then type "Ctrl-L"). You may want to go into the Loop Construction view to tweak the slice points so that pitch-stretching is available over the widest possible range, but Sonar's default loop points will likely do a decent job.

TURNING MULTITRACK DRUM LIBRARIES INTO LOOPS

Several drum libraries are available in multitrack form from companies like Wizoo, Discrete Drums, East-West, Reel Drums, etc. Although these are sold on the basis of being useable out of the box for drum parts (with the additional advantage of being mixable), I see them more as a gold mine of raw materials for creating custom drum loops. Being able to process individual tracks separately is certainly a major advantage when deriving loops from multitracked parts.

For example, I did a "remix" of the Discrete Drums sample library for the company, who had received numerous requests for "dirtier," lower-resolution versions aimed for more hardcore hip-hop and dance musicians. Sonar is an ideal tool for doing this type of remixing.

The Discrete Drums drum parts all have eight tracks. Upon opening Sonar, I selected "Create a New Project" and the "8 Track Audio" template, then dragged the eight tracks over from the CD-ROM of samples to the Clips Pane. They all fell seamlessly into the eight Sonar tracks, ready for editing.

Next was to set the project tempo to that of the drum samples. Because the Discrete Drum samples were played by a human drummer, it sometimes took a little tempo tweaking to get measure markers to line up with downbeats.

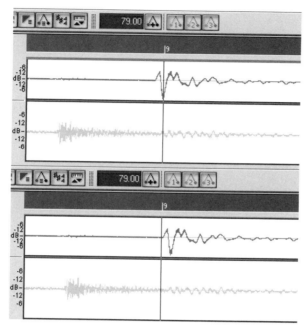

The stated file tempo was 79 BPM, but in the top window, notice how the downbeat at the beginning of measure 9 (the loop end point in this particular case) hits a little early compared to the measure marker. Changing the tempo to 79.03 BPM places the measure marker at the very beginning of the downbeat.

Furthermore, aside from some fills and such, the main groups of the Discrete Drums samples last the length of a typical chorus, verse, etc. These are usually longer than desired for a loop, so a little trimming is necessary. The easiest way is to set the Now Time at the desired loop end (snapping to grid is a good idea here), do a "Select All" (type "Ctrl-A") on the tracks, then type "S" (for Split) at the Now Time. Discard all audio to the right of the split. If necessary, repeat this process for the loop beginning.

At this point, you need to loop each track if you want to be able to change the tempo or create an Acidized file. Usually, all that's necessary is to open up

---

the Loop Construction window, specify the loop's number of beats, set "Slicing" to 16th Notes, and "Trans Detect" to 0%. This is a good default setting, but if you need to tweak it further to eliminate "flamming" or be able to stretch over the widest possible range, see "Perfecting Groove Clips" at the beginning of this chapter, which describes how to optimize slice marker placement for optimum tempo-stretching.

The next step is to test the looping by playing the Clip in loop mode to hear whether the transition is seamless or not. I usually add a 4 ms fade-out to eliminate clicks from offending tracks, and if absolutely necessary, a 2-4 ms fade-in.

Set the loop tempo as desired, confirm that all is well, then Export Audio (see the chapter on Exporting Files)—instant loop!

LOOP RECORDING À LA SONAR

Loop recording is one of the best arguments yet for hard disk recording. I love the idea of playing a part as many times as necessary to get some solid takes, then piecing together the best bits from the various takes to create a perfect composite part. Sonar makes it easy to do loop recording, but there are some ambiguities in the documentation that could cause confusion. Here's the loop recording process in a nutshell.

1. Set the loop points. I find it easiest to set "Snap to Grid" to 1 measure, drag across the time line for the appropriate number of measures, then click on the "Set Loop to Selection" button. By the way, always allow a few measures before and after the part to give the performer a little "down time" before doing another performance. You'll get fresher takes.
2. Go *Transport > Record Options.*

Before getting into loop recording, choose the way you want your tracks stored. In this case, "Store Takes in Separate Tracks" has been selected. "Recording Mode" options matter only if you select "Store Takes in a Single Track."

3. Choose the Loop Recording mode. "Store Takes in a Single Track" stacks all the takes on one track, which is a tidy way to do things, but ultimately will require you to move them to separate tracks anyway for editing. "Store Takes in Separate Tracks" creates a consecutive series of tracks, adding a new track for each pass. Any existing tracks are "pushed down" to make room for the new tracks.
4. If you chose "Store Takes in Separate Tracks," you're done. Click on "OK."
5. If you chose "Store Takes in a Single Track," decide whether consecutive loops will overwrite previous takes or be stacked on top of each other (you will not hear previous takes when you stack takes).
6. To overwrite a previous take, click on "Overwrite." To Stack takes, click on "Sound on Sound."
7. You're done; click on "OK."

The prep work is now done. I recommend using "Overwrite" only if you like to record lots of material at a time—like letting the recorder run when you're jamming on some ideas, where long periods of time might pass before there's anything work keeping. This way you won't keep gobbling up hard disk space.

But there's a major caution with overwrite: A new loop erases the *entire* previous take the instant it starts looping. If you've done something you want to keep, immediately click on "Stop" so the recording process doesn't loop back to the beginning.

Use "Store Takes in Separate Tracks" if you don't do huge numbers of overdubs. This saves the step of moving tracks around for editing. But if you're the kind of person who likes to pile on 20 takes, you might want to choose "Sound on Sound" and "Store Takes in Single Track." That way you can pull three or four out at a time, isolate the best parts, then pull out some more and work on them.

One final hint: Although you can erase the most recent take by choosing *Transport > Reject Loop Take* or pressing "Ctrl + Spacebar," this works only for MIDI tracks, not audio.

CHANGING THE LOOP PLAYBACK DEFAULT

While we're on the subject of looping, the program defaults to continuous looping when looping is active. But if you stop in the middle of the loop, the Now Time stays where you stopped. I prefer transports to do this except while looping, when it's better if the Now Time snaps back to the loop beginning when you stop.

There's a quick way to fix this:

1. Go *Transport > Loop and Auto Shuttle.*
2. Check "Stop at the End Time and Rewind to Start."
3. Click on "OK."

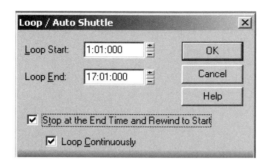

This dialog box allows having the Now Time rewind to the loop start whenever you stop the Transport.

Note that this works not only for playback but for recording, where returning to the beginning after stopping is even more important.

4

PLUG-INS

Plug-ins are one of the most exciting developments to hit hard disk record-ing since its inception. After all, how else could you have a rack of synths and processors that take up no space, don't need a power supply, and have their presets saved automatically with a song? Let's investigate how to get the most out of this wonderful new technology.

SAVE CPU POWER BY "FREEZING" PLUG-INS

Even the most macho computers can't run a sophisticated hard disk recorder along with loads of processor-hogging virtual effects and synthesizers. Although there's been quite a buzz about the "freeze" feature that saves con-siderable CPU power in other programs, Sonar users have been doing this for years—it just requires a little user assembly.

The idea behind "freezing" is to premix the CPU-intensive track into a hard disk audio track (which requires less CPU power than a track with real-time plug-ins), then disconnect the plug-ins from the CPU.

In the following, we'll assume your instrument has already been inserted (therefore, there's an audio track for the output, and a MIDI track for the part triggering the instrument), and the MIDI part has been recorded and edited as desired. First, we'll do the premix.

Creating a Premix

1. Solo both the instrument and MIDI track, and Ctrl-click on their track numbers so that they are both selected.
2. Play the part, and check for proper levels on the instrument track and the bus it's feeding. As usual, you want to get the levels as close as pos-sible to 0 without hitting it.

3. Once the levels are correct, select *Edit > Bounce to Track(s)*.
4. Tell the dialog box what track number to use, and its source bus (e.g., the audio bus fed by the instrument). Leave all the Mix Enable boxes checked, and set Separation to "Each Main Out to Separate Submix."
5. Click on "OK," and Sonar creates a hard disk audio track from the instrument output.
6. For convenience, move this track in the Track Pane (click in the empty space to the right of the track's name, and drag) so it's close to the related instrument and MIDI tracks.

Freezing and Unfreezing the Plug-Ins

Right-click on the track number of the source track containing the virtual instrument, and select "Archive." (Note that archiving is *not* the same as muting. With muting, the track is still "connected" because it needs to be able to play back instantly when unmuted.) An "A" replaces the Mute button's "M" to indicate "archive." This process disconnects the track and any associated plug-ins from the CPU, so you now need to monitor the premixed track instead of the original. Also, the instrument's corresponding MIDI track will be archived if the virtual instrument was inserted using the *Insert > DXi Synth* command.

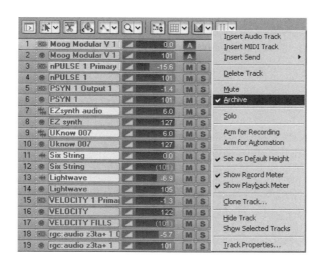

Archiving a soft synth track reduces CPU drain considerably.

To "unfreeze" the original track (*e.g.*, you want to do more editing on it), right-click and uncheck the "Archive" option. Don't forget to Mute, Archive, or discard the premixed track so you don't hear both tracks playing back at once. In any event, keep the MIDI part; it requires virtually no memory or CPU power, so should you later decide to change the instrument part, you can just do the following.:

1. Mute the hard disk audio track, or erase it if you're certain you won't use it.
2. Re-enable the instrument by right-clicking in the title bar of its associated audio track, and uncheck "Archive."
3. Edit or re-play the MIDI part, then follow the steps given earlier to create the new hard disk track.

LOAD MORE PLUG-INS

The more plug-ins you insert, the harder your CPU has to work. If the CPU activity meter spends more time on the right side than the left, you've probably wished you could upgrade your CPU. But there's a simpler way to load more plug-ins: Increase the latency.

Lower latency settings are desirable because, among other reasons, they give a more responsive feel when playing soft synths—it's no fun to play a note, then hear it with an audible delay. In fact, one of the great things about WDM and ASIO drivers is that it's possible to obtain ultra-low latencies. For example, my system works very reliably with around 3 ms of latency.

However, increasing the latency to 11 ms dramatically lowers the CPU load, allowing the use of more plug-ins. Yet the loss of response isn't too bad; just to put things in perspective, a latency of 11 ms would have been hailed as a breakthrough not all that long ago.

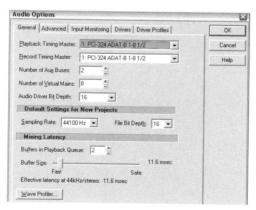

The minimum available latency is 2.9 ms, but here the buffer size has been increased to 11.6 ms to allow loading lots of soft synths and other plug-ins. Note this system uses MOTU's original 2408 interface with the PCI-324 card; contrary to internet rumors, its WDM drivers get along just fine with Sonar and other Windows XP programs.

To change the latency setting (this can be done at any time, you don't need to reboot), go *Options > Audio*. In the Mixing Latency section, adjust the "Buffers in Playback Queue" or "Buffer Size" parameters to change latency. Increasing either the buffer size or the number of buffers produces similar end results, however with my system the CPU stresses out less if I increase buffer size and keep a small number of buffers in the playback queue. Specifically, my "low latency" setting is 2 buffers with a buffer size of 2.9 ms. The "let's be nice to the CPU" setting is 2 buffers with a buffer size of 11.6 ms.

DON'T FORGET ABOUT FREEBIES

There are quite a few free plug-ins floating around the web, but one of my favorites is the free DXi version of the Triangle II softsynth from **www.rgcaudio.com**. It's only 2.5MB, so it doesn't even take much download time. This mono synth sounds great for lead and bass lines, incorporates processing (delay, feedback, distortion, chorus, bass boost, and bit reduction), and even includes a lot of useful presets.

The Triangle II synth is available in a DXi version for Sonar. It's only a monophonic synth, but the programming options are excellent, as is the sound quality.

The best part: Shift-right click on a parameter, and the synth goes into "Learn" mode so you can use your keyboard's knobs and data sliders (providing they transmit MIDI data, of course) to control various Triangle II parameters in real time. You can also set minimum and maximum control excursions, and reverse the control's action. This is one hot little freebie, but be forewarned—this is likely to make you covet the more advanced Pentagon synth, which is not free.

MAKING THE MOST OF VST ADAPTER

Sonar's plug-in architecture was originally designed to accommodate DirectX plug-ins for signal processing (including automatable DirectX 8-compatible effects), as well as DXi plug-in software synths. However, "wrappers" have existed for Sonar that allow VST devices (processors and soft synths) to appear as DX devices, and can therefore work within Sonar. The wrapper concept took a giant leap forward when Cakewalk purchased the technology for VST Adapter and started including it with Sonar.

I'm always surprised at how well "wrapped" VST plug-ins work with Sonar. There appears to be no serious performance hit or increase in latency—in fact, some VST plug-ins running under a wrapper offer functions not available in DX plug-ins. However, there are nonetheless rare instances where a plug-in just won't work properly. And sometimes, certain features aren't handled correctly, like when you try to arm an instrument for automation and instead of seeing a tidy list of parameters, there's a blank window, or worse yet, gibberish. But overall wrappers work amazingly well, given the complexity of the task they're asked to perform.

However, no wrapper can translate VST variants that are keyed to a particular program. For example, Cubase SX has some VST effects that won't work in other VST hosts, let alone with a wrapper.

How VST-DX Adapter Operates

All wrapper programs need to know where to look for plug-ins. As I also have Cubase SX installed on my machine, a folder loaded with VST plug-ins already exists, so I load new plug-ins in there, and direct the wrapper to find its plug-ins there. If you haven't installed any VST hosts, you'll need to create a folder for VST plug-ins.

With VST Adapter, you invoke a configuration program (dsecribed in the next section, "Synching VST Effects to Tempo") that allows several options. It scans the folders you selected, then creates a list of available plug-ins, along with data about them. You can select individual plug-ins and specify characteristics unique to them. For example, one soft synth opens up to a small "macro" screen, and when you try to access larger pages, the window may remain limited to the macro screen size. In VST Adapter, you can specify a fixed Editor size in pixels to accommodate this. Note that you need to re-run the configuration program whenever you add a new VST effect.

VST Plug-In Search Paths

Please select the folder(s) in which VST plug-ins are stored on your system. The Wizard will search these folders and all their subfolders.

C:\Program Files\Steinberg\Vstplugins

Add... Remove Folder defaults... Reset all...

Options
☐ Re-scan failed plug-ins
☐ Re-scan existing plug-ins   ☐ Don't add VST prefix

Next > Cancel

When you run VST Adapter's configuration routine, there are several options (such as forcing a re-scan of plug-ins that won't load, just in case they load properly when queried again), and you can also set default characteristics. After VST Adapter compiles its list of plug-ins, it's possible to change the default characteristics individually for each plug-in. For example, you might want one plug-in to respond to external MIDI Controllers, while another responds to external NRPN data.

Synching VST Effects to Tempo

VST effects that sync to tempo perfectly with VST hosts may appear not to sync properly with Sonar. Fortunately, there's an easy solution.

VST Adapter operates under a few assumptions, and one is that effects capable of synching to the host tempo are instruments. Therefore, if you register these types of effects as DXi instruments, they will follow tempo. Note, however, that these devices will show up under "DXi Instruments" when you go to insert them.

To register a plug-in as a DXi instrument, go *Programs > Cakewalk > Cakewalk VST Adapter 4 > Cakewalk VST Adapter 4.* Click "Next" when the Welcome screen appears, then "Next" again when the Adapter shows the search paths.

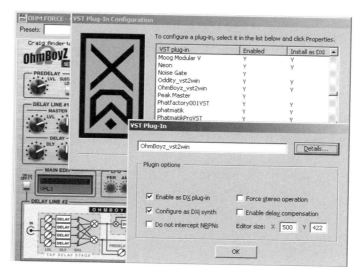

Cakewalk's VST Adapter 4 allows changing the properties of registered plug-ins, including treating audio effects like DXi devices capable of synching to the host's tempo.

The adapter scans the target VST plug-ins folder for devices, then presents them all in a list. Scroll down to the plug-in you want to register as a DXi, click on it, then click on Properties. Check the box that says "Configure as DXi Synth," then click on "OK."

Click on "Next," and wait while VST Adapter registers all the available plug-ins. When it's done, click on "Finish." To insert the effect, right-click in a track's effects slot but instead of choosing Audio Effects, look in the DXi Synths list, and you'll see the effect located there. When inserted, it should now follow any tempo changes within Sonar.

About Multiple Outputs and Arming Parameters

VST Adapter can recognize instruments with multiple outputs, but note that there are two ways to install soft synths:

• Create an audio track, right-click on its FX slot and select the instru-ment, then create a MIDI track and assign its output to drive the instru-ment. This approach allows only stereo outs. However, it is the only mode that allows using an instrument as a signal processor (*e.g.*, the rotating speaker section of Native Instruments' B4).

- Go *Insert > DXi Synth* and choose the instrument you want to insert. This installs the synth in the "Synth Rack View," and presents an options screen that allows choosing "All Synth Outputs," which will create an audio track for each instrument output (you can also specify just the main synth output, which is typically stereo). In this case, the instrument resides in the synth rack and has an associated audio track, but the track's FX slot doesn't have an instrument in it.

With DXi instruments, the Insert approach is recommended. But with VST instruments, unless you need the multiple outputs, use the first method and load them into the FX slot. This way, if you right-click on the instrument's name and select "Arm Parameter," in most cases this will bring up a list of parameters that can be armed for automation.

When you arm parameters and click on the toolbar's Record Automation button, you can move the on-screen controls corresponding to the armed parameters, and their motion will create track envelopes in the audio track. These can be edited further if desired.

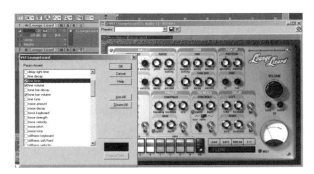

If you try to arm parameters for a VST device loaded in the FX slot, most of the time you'll see a list of parameters, and boxes you can check to determine which parameters will be recorded when you move their corresponding control. This particular automation option is not possible with DXi synthesizers, although it does work well with automatable effects, including VST effects run through a wrapper. The screen shot shows the Lounge Lizard electric piano plug-in from Applied Acoustics Systems.

Sometimes, though, there won't be a list (just boxes), or there may be nothing at all. In this case, select "Arm All" and see if that works. Be forewarned, though, that today's virtual synths may have hundreds of parameters, and arming them all might slow things down to the point where you think you have a 50 MHz 486 running the show (when you're done, be sure to select "Disarm All").

For situations where arming and moving parameters doesn't work, note that in most cases you can also right-click in the audio track itself (go *Envelopes > Create Track Envelope > click on instrument name*), and then create envelopes for editing specific parameters on a non-real time basis.

DXi devices *can* be designed so that control motions are recorded as MIDI data in the MIDI track driving the instrument. Unfortunately, few DXi instruments have this capability at present (the DreamStation DXi2 and Edirol VSC included with Sonar do). However, there's an easy, and in some ways better, workaround: If a DXi device responds to external MIDI controllers, you can use an external MIDI fader or control box (*e.g.*, Peavey PC-1600X, Kenton control boxes, Event EZ-Bus, etc.) to change the parameters in real time using hardware, and record this as MIDI data in the MIDI track. I find this more satisfying than grabbing a knob with a mouse anyway, as it's not only more efficient (you can control multiple parameters at once), but has a better "feel."

ASSIGNABLE FX CONTROLS

In Sonar Producer Edition, there are four horizontal sliders below the FX slot (in the Console view and Inspector) that can be assigned to any four FX parameters. To see these sliders, you may need to click on the FX button in the "toolbar" toward the left of the Console, or at the bottom of the Inspector strip. If the "FX" button is yellow, you'll see only the FX slot; if it's blue, the faders will show up too.

If there are several plug-ins, click on the one you want to adjust, and the four sliders will relate to the selected plug-ins. A few older plug-ins that cannot have parameters automated will not show any parameters, but most will, including VST types and DXi/VSTi soft synths.

Click on a plug-in to display four assignable, adjustable, automatable parameters. These controls can be reassigned to other parameters as needed.

The default for the four controls is the first four parameters in the list that comes up when you select "Arm Parameter" (for automation). However, you can reassign these sliders to any of a plug-in's automatable parameters. Right-click on the slider, select "Reassign Control," and choose from the list of available parameters. Thus, you don't have to leave the Console view to adjust or automate crucial parameters. For example, if you have compression plugged in to a track, you can assign "Threshold," "Compression Amount," "Output Level," and "Attack" to these knobs, making it easy to adjust parameters in context with other tracks—no "window flipping." Better yet, you can also enable remote MIDI control for these parameters, which is a boon to those of us who favor using control surfaces.

What with EQ and effects being adjustable from the mixer, the Console becomes a far friendlier mixing environment.

INSTALLING "LEGACY" PLUG-INS

To insure compatibility with older files, Sonar always includes older versions of plug-ins with the installation CD. However, only the latest set of recommended plug-ins are installed by default; you have to specifically install the legacy plug-ins.

To do this, proceed as if you're going to install Sonar, but when you get to the "Select Components" screen, click on the "Options" box for the plug-ins category. Check the boxes for any of the older plug-ins you want to install.

Click on "OK," then continue with the installation process. Next time you open Sonar, the older plug-ins will show up under the available options.

VIRTUAL INSTRUMENT TIPS

Virtual instruments are pretty amazing devices, as they put a complete synthesizer, sampler, drum machine, guitar emulator, or whatever right inside your computer—no rack space (or wall wart power supply!) required. Sonar comes with several instruments, and plenty more are available. Here are some tips on how to use virtual instruments.

Cyclone DXi, the Groove Soft Synth

Sonar 2.0 saw the introduction of Cyclone, a "groove"-oriented DXi with deep applications for loop-based music. The printed page is inadequate to fully show how cool this thing is, so you can go through the following tutorial to hear it for yourself. You can use any two Acidized WAV files or Groove Clips;

we'll call one YIN.WAV and the other YANG.WAV. For best results, these should be drum grooves.

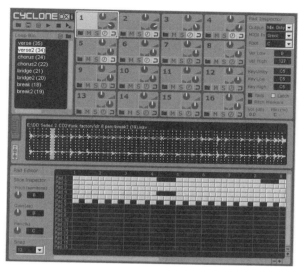

Cyclone is a DXi instrument that's ideal for groove applications. The loop bin toward the left holds the acidized loops that Cyclone uses; the 16 pads control playback, and the Pad Inspector toward the right controls pad characteristics (such as velocity triggering, keyrange, output channel, and the like). The strip in the middle shows the waveform and the Acidizing markers for the highlighted file in the Loop Bin, while the Pad Editor at the bottom allows rearranging, cutting, pasting, and moving the "grains" that make up the loops.

1. Open Sonar. Select "Create a New Project" from the Quick Start menu, select "Normal," name the Project if you save projects on a per-project basis, then click on "OK." The Normal template Track View appears. Set the tempo to 120 BPM or so.
2. Go *Insert > DXi Synth > Cyclone*. In the Options box, check "MIDI Source Track," "First Synth Output," and "Synth Property Page." Leave "Synth Rack View" unchecked, then click on "OK."
3. An audio track appears called "Cyclone 1 Mix," along with an accompanying MIDI track and the Cyclone instrument window.
4. In Cyclone's Loop Bin, click on the folder icon and navigate to the location of the two files. Double-click on YIN.WAV.
5. Repeat step 4, but double-click on YANG.WAV. Both files should now show up in the Loop Bin.
6. Drag YIN.WAV from the loop bin onto one of the pad "tracks" in the Pad Editor toward the bottom of the window, then similarly drag YANG.WAV onto another track.

7. There are 16 pads. Click on Pad 1. This loop will keep playing because the loop button is enabled (enabling the Sync to Tempo "clock" button means that it follows the project tempo). This pad is in latch mode (the Latch button in the Pad Inspector glows green), so you click once to turn on, and once to turn off.
8. Now click on Pad 2 at the downbeat of a measure. It will start playing with the Pad 1 loop.
9. Click on the keyboard button just underneath the Loop Bin, toward the left. Pads can also be triggered from individual keyboard keys; this window shows which MIDI keys trigger which pads. There's a lot of flexibility here—you can transpose sounds, trigger them over a range of keys, and do other tricks. But we're on a different mission here, so consult the manual for more info on using a keyboard with Cyclone.
10. Turn off both pads. Note the lower window shows the individual "grains" that make up each sound. Click on the "Auto Preview" button (the right arrow/little speaker, just below the DXi logo next to the Cyclone logo) to hear grains as you click on them. Note that you can zoom horizontally and vertically in this window, as needed.
11. In the Pad Editor, click on some of the Pad 1 grains and drag them to Pad 3's track. Do the same for some of the grains from Pad 2, until you've created a new loop for Pad 3. Play Pad 3 to hear what you've created.
12. You can Crtl-drag grains to copy them, and stack multiple grains in one slot. Even better, each grain has adjustable pitch, gain, and pan controls.

This just scratches the surface of what Cyclone can do, so take the time to play around with it a bit and get familiar with its talents. Meanwhile, when you want to get back to a clean slate and clear the contents of a Cyclone DXi project, click the Trash icon in the DXi toolbar. All the loops will be deleted from your project.

Exploiting Edirol VSC Automation

Don't dismiss the Edirol VSC soft synth just because it was included free with Sonar. Not only can it make some decent sounds and not drain a lot of power, but it also handles basic automation functions. For example, you can tweak VSC faders and record the movements as automation data for volume, pan, expression, reverb send, chorus send, and delay send.

To do this, click on "Setup" in the VSC's lower right corner and go to the "Misc." tab. Check the "Record VSC Panel Operations" box.

Now arm the VSC's corresponding MIDI control track for recording (not automation, just recording), go into record, and move the faders around as desired. On playback, the faders will move to reflect the automation data.

The VSC will respond to even more parameters using envelopes. Right-click on the VSC's MIDI track in the Clips View, and go *Envelopes > Create Track Envelopes > MIDI*. Click on the "Value" drop-down menu, and you'll see a list of automatable parameters. These include the ones that can be recorded from the front panel, but also, several others such as filter resonance, brightness, decay time, etc.

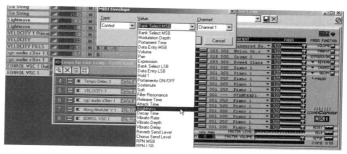

Right-clicking on the Edirol VSC's MIDI track leads to the Envelope options, where you can create track envelopes for various VSC parameters. In this example, "Brightness" is being selected.

Edirol VSC Multiple Outputs

In addition to automation, the VSC can provide four discrete outputs if you specify "All Synth Outputs" in the Insert DXi Synth Options dialog box that opens up when you insert a DXi synth. To assign channels (parts) to these outs, click on the VSC's "Setup" button, go to the "Output Assign" tab, and assign the desired part to the desired output. Each out will be represented by an audio track in the Tracks Pane.

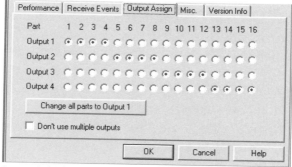

Any of the VSC's 16 parts (which correspond to MIDI channels) can go to any of the four available audio outputs. If multiple parts feed multiple outs, they'll be layered together—great for layering parts that you want to process with the same effects.

Sonar's Groove Module: Arturia Storm

Cyclone is a fun groove module, but Sonar has no TB-303-type devices or synth/pattern generator combinations.

One possible solution, as described in more detail later, is to use the ReWire protocol to insert other programs like Cakewalk Project5, Propellerhead Reason, etc. into Sonar. However, there's also a very inexpensive option: Arturia's Storm 2.0. For under $100, you get 11 instruments (analog bass line synth, modeled bass, two tone generators optimized for chord generating, five drum sets each with different "kits," polyphonic synthesizer, and "scratching" module with two virtual turntables). I'm not counting Storm's recording modules, which are redundant with Sonar. There are also ten effects (chorus, compressor, distortion, dual delays, flanger, low pass filter, reverb, ring modulator, sequencer filter, and vocoder).

Storm can ReWire into Sonar, but the implementation is not as flexible as when you use it as a VST instrument with ASIO. Incidentally, a two-monitor setup really helps, as you can set up Storm in its own screen.

After installing Storm and registering it with VST Adapter, go *Insert > DXi Synth > VST > Storm,* (make sure the box that says "All Synth Outputs" is checked), and Storm will connect into the system, with each of its four instruments grabbing four Sonar tracks. The "primary" (master) channel also grabs a track, but this should be used only for adding in effects, as bringing it up the same time as individual channels causes nasty comb filtering (more on this later). The Insert process also creates a MIDI source track. Note that you must define some sort of region before Storm will play, as pressing "Play" on Sonar starts triggering Storm's loop generators. If there's no area to loop in, they get upset.

Now here's the best part: You can play the instruments via MIDI. Right-click on the blank part of a Storm instrument, select MIDI configuration, check On, and choose the desired channel. Set that same channel number in the MIDI track's Ch parameter (Out should of course be set to Storm). Set the instruments to different channels, and select the one you want to play at Sonar's MIDI track. You may want to create additional MIDI tracks so that each instrument has its own track, with its own assignment. You can play the drums too; just clear any existing pattern and "play in" the part.

Ctrl-clicking on a Storm instrument knob specifies how it will respond to MIDI controller signals; you can enter the channel and controller number manually, or just click on Learn, diddle the control you want to use to drive Storm, and let Storm do the hard work. If you put Sonar into record, it will record whatever control signals you put it into, thus automating Storm's sound on playback.

Storm can be used as a VST instrument with Sonar. Here you can see how Storm has grabbed five audio tracks and one MIDI track; also note how one of the knobs on the Bass 52 module has been selected for MIDI control, which brings up a dialog box where you can enter the controller number/channel or go into Learn mode.

Not enough control? You can also create envelopes in the MIDI tracks. If you want to know what value controller you should enter for the envelope, no problem—just Ctrl-click on the parameter you want to control, and it will show the existing assignment.

There are some issues with using Storm's effects, though. I recommend turning all the Dry controls to zero, as that prevents any straight instrument signal from getting into the primary track. Then, use the remaining sends to determine the strength of the effect you want to add. The effect outs will show up in the master track, and its fader can now serve as a master effects return control. What makes this all the more fun is that the send and effects parameters can be automated as well.

Storm is fairly processor-hungry, so after creating a loop or section with it, I'll usually bounce the results to a hard disk track. You can solo individual tracks to save out elements of the loop individually.

Beefier DreamStation Sounds

The CPU-friendly DreamStation synth has been a fixture of Sonar since version 1.0. While it is easy to program and automate, I've never heard its sound described as "thrilling." But it can do some decent bass lines, and this trick tells how make them a bit more dramatic. This technique applies to other synths as well, but you can get away with layering a fair number of DreamStations before your CPU reports you to the authorities for processor abuse.

The idea is to layer two bass sounds with different velocity responses. One synth provides the main bass sound, and has no velocity response, so it plays at the same level regardless of velocity. The second synth, with a harder or more percussive sound, has full velocity response so that the higher the velocity, the louder it sounds. Thus, if you play a part that accents particular notes, the second bass will come into play with those notes.

To do this, we'll take advantage of Sonar's ability to drive multiple synths on different tracks simultaneously. Insert the two synths you want to layer, and turn Input Echo On for both tracks. As you play your keyboard, you should hear both synths layered together.

On your main DreamStation, adjust the Amplifier (envelope) Gain control to 100%. On the second DreamStation, set the Amplifier Gain control to 0%. This provides maximum velocity scaling of the amplitude envelope.

Record enable both MIDI tracks, and start recording while playing a highly dynamic part. The overall sound should be a lot more interesting.

You can also use this technique on mixdown if you've already recorded a synth, but want to layer another one for a more dramatic effect. Insert the second synth into an audio track (right-click on the FX slot, go "DXi Synth," then choose the desired instrument), clone the MIDI track, and assign the cloned MIDI track's output to the synth you just inserted. Adjust controls on both synths as described previously, and now you can give your bass part a boost on mixdown.

Two DreamStations have been layered on separate tracks. By turning on Thru and record-enabling both MIDI tracks, you can play into both synths simultaneously while recording into their respective tracks.

SIGNAL PROCESSING PLUG-IN TIPS

Signal processors started the plug-in movement, and the latest edition of Sonar includes lots of useful, automatable, great-sounding processors. It's also wonderful to have access to the world of VST processors, as well. So, let's plug in and check out some of the tricks Sonar can do with processors. Revealing All the EQ

If you use Sonar Producer, you've no doubt enjoyed having built-in 4-stage EQ in every track and bus in the Console view. However, although the Console view shows only four bands, the EQs being used are the same six-band Sonitus fx:Equalizer plug-ins that show up under audio effects. To access the other two bands, make sure the console's EQ plot (thumbnail graph) is visible. If not, click on the Plot button (the one that looks somewhat like a sine wave) in the toolbar to the left of the console.

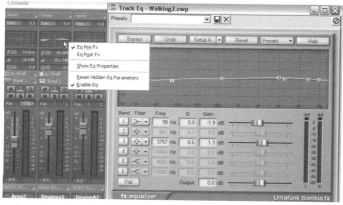

Although you only see four bands of EQ in the console, it's possible to access another two bands, as well as place the EQ pre or post effects.

Double-click on a plot (or right-click on it and select "Show Eq Properties"). If the EQ in that channel is enabled (in other words, the on-off button toward the bottom of the EQ section glows green), then the full plug-in will appear. You can now enable and adjust bands 5 and 6. Note that any changes you make to the EQ will show up in the response plot, even though you can't access these two bands directly from the Console view.

The menu that pops up when you right-click on the plot has some other useful options. One is to place the EQ pre or post effects, and another resets all hidden EQ parameters (i.e., bands 5 and 6).

Wahwah of the Disco Gods

One of Sonar Producer's plug-ins is the Sonitus fx:wahwah. You can sweep the wa frequency manually, trigger it for envelope effects, or have it sweep in time with a settable tempo. However, if you want to get into the real spirit of wah funkification, you'll want to be able to control the sweep with a foot pedal...and unfortunately, although fx:wahwah's frequency can be envelope-controlled, you can't assign it to a remote control and rock out.

There's a workaround, though: Use Sonar Producer's built-in parametric EQ. But you'll also need some special mojo, as just turning up the parametric's resonance and sweeping the frequency doesn't sound like a real wahwah. That's because a parametric has a flat response, with the peak poking above it. A real wa-wa rejects frequencies around the resonant peak so you don't hear anything except the peak.

So, here's the secret way to get the Shaft-approved "Gods of Disco" wahwah sound. Begin by cloning the track to which you want to add the effect, then invert the phase (Ø symbol) of one of the tracks. Now click on Play; you won't hear anything, because the two tracks cancel each other out. You can verify this by changing the level slightly on one of the tracks, at which point you'll hear audio. Return to the original level.

Now turn on one band of Peak/Dip EQ for *one* of the channels. As a starting point, set Q = 3.3, boost = 12 dB, and vary the frequency between about 200 Hz to 1.5 kHz. You should hear the cool wahwah sound. (If you solo the track that has the parametric, the authentic wahwah sound goes away, replaced by an ordinary-sounding parametric sweep.)

The secret to getting a great wahwah sound is to duplicate a channel, throw it out of phase, and vary a parametric's peak frequency on only one of the channels.

Next, let's control the parametric frequency with a footpedal, mod wheel, etc. Right-click on the EQ's frequency parameter, and select "Remote Control." In the dialog box that appears, enter the MIDI message you want to use. If you don't know what it is, just diddle your controller then click on "Learn." For example, if you want to control a parameter with your synth's footpedal (assuming it outputs MIDI data) but aren't sure what controller number it generates, click on "Learn" *while* you move the pedal.

Arm the parameter for automation, and begin automation recording. Work that footpedal, and when you're done, click on "Stop."

If you have the Studio Edition without the built-in EQ (or a previous version of Sonar), all is not lost: You can get pretty much the same sound by inserting an FxEq plug-in into one of the channels, and adjusting the controls as described above. However, like the fx:wahwah, the frequency can only be envelope-controlled.

Fortunately, there is a workaround—albeit a not totally satisfactory one—for doing foot control of either the fx:wahwah wa parameter or FxEq frequency. Assign a parameter that can respond to remote control, such as pan or aux send, to your pedal. Next, record automation, and move the pedal the way you would for a wahwah part. Of course you won't hear the wah changes, but at least we're partway to a solution.

When you're done recording the foot pedal-generated automation envelope, right-click on the envelope, choose "Assign Envelope," and assign it to the fx:wahwah wa parameter or FxEq frequency, depending on which you used. On playback, the parameter will respond to the foot controller messages.

Re-Amping with Sonar

Wouldn't it be great if you could choose a guitar's amp tone *while mixing down* instead of being locked in to the tone you used while recording? Well it is great, and thanks to plug-in technology, fast computers, and Sonar's ability to monitor a track input, it's possible as well.

For years, engineers and guitarists have used a technique called "re-amping." With this, a guitarist splits the guitar signal in two: One feed goes direct to an amp, and the other goes straight into the recorder via a direct box. As the guitarist plays, the amp signal is recorded—but so is the straight signal, on a separate track.

During mixdown, if the amp track sounds fine, that's great. But if not, the engineer can mute the amp track, feed the straight track's output into a different amp, then record the output of the other amp. Or, another option is to keep the original amp track, but add a new amp track to provide stereo or layered effects.

Sonar allows a new twist on the traditional re-amping concept. With older, slower audio interfaces, monitoring through plug-ins was impractical due to latency. However, with today's fast computers and improved drivers, the latency added by going through a plug-in running in Sonar, even when added to the conversion latency, can still be well under 3-4 ms. To put things in perspective, 3 ms of latency is about the same amount of delay as if you moved your head a yard further away from your amp—not really enough to affect the "feel" of your playing.

In my experience, if the overall latency is less than 5 ms, playing through a plug-in will not be a problem. In the range of 5-10 ms, you might find the amount of delay disconcerting. Above 10 ms, this technique doesn't really work because your playing comes back to you like slapback echo. In this case, I suggest using traditional re-amping techniques.

Best of all, the key to what makes "virtual re-amping" possible is that Sonar records the straight guitar signal to the track, not the version through the plug-in. So, any processing that occurs depends entirely on the plug-in(s) you've selected; you can process the guitar in any way you'd like during the mixdown process, including changing "virtual amps," patching in high-quality reverb, or whatever.

Here's how to proceed.

1. Check that there is no feedback loop from the host output back to the input. To be safe, turn down your monitor speakers.
2. Feed the instrument to be virtually re-amped into the desired audio track by choosing the appropriate hardware input.
3. Enable the driver for the desired input (under *Audio Options > Drivers*).
4. Turn on the "Input Echo" function (in the Tracks Pane, click on the button to the right of the "Record" button). It will glow green.
5. Enable the track's "Record" button. You should hear your input source.
6. Insert the plug-in(s) of your choice into the FX slot.
7. Your input source will play through the plug-in, and assuming a fast sound card with decent drivers, latency will be either very small or insignificant...so start recording!

This shot shows IK Multimedia's AmpliTube inserted as a real-time effect into Sonar. The outstanding feature of taking this approach is that the straight guitar signal is recorded—not the processed one—so you can process it any way you want during mixdown.

Although we've presented input monitoring in a guitar re-amping context, monitoring through plug-ins has other uses:

• Vocalists often like to hear themselves with compression, reverb, EQ, etc. while singing. By monitoring through Sonar, they can hear what their voice will sound like through particular plug-ins. And of course, these can be changed on mixdown.

- Session musicians aren't forced to bring their effects racks or other processors; they can use plug-ins within Sonar.
- Bassists are used to recording direct, but with this technique, they can monitor through more of an amp sound.
- Using an effect like tempo-synched delay on a drummer will influence how the part is played. By monitoring through Sonar, the drummer can hear the effect the delay will have on the drum part, and play accordingly.

The SpectraFX

SpectraFX is an X/Y controller with effects, sort of like Korg's KAOSS pad, that you can control with a mouse or joystick. It also has an autosweep function that can sync to tempo, as well as follow envelopes recorded or drawn into a track. Sonar can also record controller movements made with the SpectraFX for use with other effects or track parameters.

To get acquainted with the SpectraFX, I suggest loading a full drum loop (i.e., lots of sounds, not just a kick or snare) into a track, and looping it for 16 measures or so. Then, right-click on the track's FX bin and go *Audio Effects > Cakewalk > SpectraFX*.

The SpectraFX is an unusual signal processor with X-Y control that can sync to beats or measures.

1. In the list of effects toward the right of the plug-in, click on "Bass Wa."
2. For the particular effect we're about to use, turn "Mix Level" fully clockwise.
3. There are three main control mechanisms: The horizontal slider along the bottom (X-axis), vertical slider along the right of the X/Y pad (Y-axis), and the locus—the little circle on the pad's surface.
4. Move the X-Axis slider all the way to the left, then start playing the loop.
5. Move the Y-Axis slider up and down; higher settings give a "peakier" sound. Leave it at the highest position.
6. Move the X-Axis slider to the right to increase the wah frequency.

7. Grab the locus (the circle in the middle) with your mouse and move it around the X/Y pad. Like other SpectraFX patches, the least "effected" sound occurs with the locus in the lower left, and the most effected sound with the locus in the upper right.

Now let's beat-sync a pattern to the effect with Autosweep.

1. Click the "Beats" button.
2. An ellipse appears with two light blue circles and two other circles.
3. Drag these circles to change the ellipse's shape.
4. The locus rotation (its "orbit") is synched to the beat. Click on the "Beat" field, and use the (-) and (+) buttons to change the time for a complete orbit. This is variable from once every beat to every 32 beats.
5. You can also sync the orbit to measures. Click on the "Meas" field, and select the number of measures, from 1 to 32. However, like the beat option, you can't choose numbers that aren't a power of two.

One cool feature is that mouse or joystick movement overrides the sync. So, you can click on the X/Y pad and drag around to change the sound at any time; release the mouse, and the effect goes back to being beat-synched.

Recording mouse/joystick movements is simple:

1. Right-click on the SpectraFX module in the FX slot and select "Arm Parameter."
2. Check "Pad X Axis" and "Pad Y Axis," assuming you want to automate both, then click on "OK."
3. Click on the "Record Automation" button in the Transport toolbar, move the locus around (or use the autosweep function), and click on "Stop" when you're done.

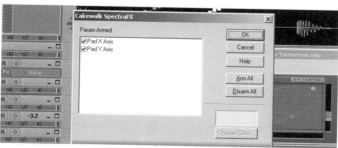

Both the X Axis and Y Axis controller motions have been armed for automation. Note the automated curves in the background; these correspond to the locus sweep. The envelopes are assignable to parameters in effects and tracks, not just the SpectraFX.

You'll now see the two envelope curves. But here's the best part: You can apply these envelopes to other parameters—right-click on the envelope, and see what's available under "Assign Envelope." This includes the usual pan, volume, aux bus send pan, aux send volume, etc., but also automatable parameters from other DirectX 8 effects. (To automate DXi instrument parameters, you first need to add the DXi envelope you want to automate to the track, then assign the SpectraFX envelope to it.)

Suffice it to say the SpectraFX is a plug-in whose usefulness goes way beyond its most obvious applications.

Emulating Room Ambiences with Short Delays

Listen to a drum machine that was recorded direct into Sonar, or a soft synth with no processing. While the sound is clean, there's also a certain deadness. The stereo is too wide, and instruments like drums become individual points of sound instead of being part of a cohesive, unified kit. Psycho-acoustically, we're still used to instruments having some "air," both from resonances within the instruments themselves and from the room in which they are played.

The Pantheon reverb is a great addition to Sonar, but it's optimized more for larger acoustical spaces and plate reverb effects. Fortunately, Sonar has some great tools if you want to experiment with modeling smaller spaces to add "room ambience." This doesn't substitute for reverb, but adds more depth and interest to the sound, even if you do add reverb afterward.

We'll start with a single FxDelay used as an aux bus effect. Try these values as a point of departure:

	Delay	Fine	Feedbk	Pan
Voice 1	0.00	5.00	10.00	-0.40
Voice 2	0.00	7.00	-10.00	-1.00
Voice 3	0.00	3.00	10.00	0.40
Voice 4	0.00	9.00	-10.00	1.00

Set "Mix Level" to 1.00 (full wet). This setup seems to work best with the short delays panned closer to center, and longer delays panned left and right. However, even small changes in pan and delay settings can make a big difference in the sound. Remember to mix in the delayed signal sparingly; play your main track, then turn up the delay bus level just enough to hear an effect.

The effect this produces is called "comb filtering," and most of the time, we don't want it in our recordings. However, this effect is so tied in with the sound of miking an instrument in a small room with hard surfaces, that psycho-acoustically a little comb filtering makes our brain says "Aha! This was recorded in a small room with hard surfaces!"

Of course, you can add even more FxDelay processors to create a more complex "room" with additional reflections. One caution: Although the whole point of this exercise is to add the phase cancellation/addition effects found in the average room, high levels of processed signal can cause excessive cancellation and "thin" the sound. At some point, check the main bus output in mono to make sure that the sound is still acceptable. The likelihood of any thinness occurring will most likely be in the bass range, so you may want to use EQ to add a slight bass "bump."

The FxChorus effect is also useful for modeling room ambience. This particular chorus has four delay lines, and no law says we *have* to use them as a straight-ahead chorus box. The main difference compared to the previous example is that the FxChorus, because of the modulation, gives a less "hard" and more diffused sound, so the "room" appears a little bigger and softer. Also, negative effects from comb filtering are less of an issue (although you should still check the master output in mono). Here are some suggested values:

	Delay	Mod Depth	Pan	Mod Freq
Voice 1	5.00	12.00	0.40	0.10
Voice 2	7.00	12.00	1.00	0.20
Voice 3	9.00	12.00	-0.40	0.30
Voice 4	11.00	12.00	-1.00	0.40

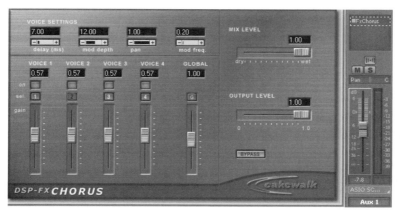

Although the FxDelay plug-in works for adding short delays to create ambience, the FxChorus also does a great job because you can add subtle modulation.

The slow modulation effect adds a bit of animation that dynamically colors the sound. To change the room characteristics, try other delay times between 1 and 15 ms, vary the modulation depth, change the modulation frequency...and remember, these parameters are automatable, so you can alter the room sound over time.

Note that with mostly mono source material, these short delay techniques will tend to give better stereo imaging. With stereo source material, using short delays may "monoize" the signal and make the stereo spread less obvious. In some situations, this is a benefit as it provides an overall sonic ambience for instruments like drums.

Parallel Effects

For parallel effects, you have two choices: Insert TC Works' FX Machine or the BIAS Vbox (these are two plug-ins that let you put effects into a matrix, thus creating parallel, series, or series/parallel configurations), or simply clone the track and insert the desired parallel effect on the clone. Mix the paralleled tracks together in the desired proportion.

Copying Effects Between Tracks

If you have an effect set up perfectly and want to apply it to another track as well, no problem. Ctrl-click on the effect's name in the FX slot, then drag it to the FX bin in the destination track while continuing to hold down the Ctrl key. Once the effect has been copied, release the Ctrl key, and the effect's front panel ("Properties page") should open.

Using the FX2 Tape Sim

One of my favorite plug-ins—and certainly one of the most underrated—is the FX2 Tape Simulator. Here are a few tips on using this beast.

- It may seem like tape simulation is something you'd want to use only for final mixes, so that the master has a "crunched" tape sound. But I find it eminently suited to individual tracks. Kick drums can become really punchy, drum loops gain level by a sort of "hard" compression, and effete basses can become aggressive and rude.
- Keep the output gain low as you tweak your sound. The key control is "Rec Level." This sets the level and hardness. The "Warmth" control adds the crunch.
- For a really crunchy sound, set "Rec Level" and "Warmth" to maximum, and pull back "Input Gain" until the degree of nastiness is just right. Finally, adjust the "Output Gain" to avoid clipping the track.

- Experiment with the "Tape Speed" and "EQ Curve" controls; they affect the overall tonality.
- One of the best uses of the Tape Sim is with a kick drum track, and the "LF Boost" switch is Cakewalk's gift to dance music kick drums. Dial up the right amount of distortion, then add some boost. The end result is a kick drum that can move mountains.
- Click the bypass switch from time to time to get a dose of reality. You might be shocked at how much you can raise the overall level without hearing objectionable levels of clipping.

Sonar's Noise Generator

Before we get off the topic of tape simulation entirely, here's one last trick to unlock Sonar's secret white noise generator.

Select an audio track for the white noise, and insert Tape Sim in the FX slot. Sonar won't let you process an empty track, so place some audio on the track. I usually copy a little piece of audio from another track, then paste it after the end of the song so it's out of the way. You generally don't want to hear anything playing while the noise is going.

Press "Play." On the Tape Sim, turn up the "Hiss" and "Output Gain" controls. Note that you will not hear hiss if "Tape Speed" is set to flat; I prefer the 7.5 ips setting, but that's a matter of taste. Try 15 and 30 as well. You should now hear the hiss.

Enable the track being "processed" for recording, go into record, and you'll record the results. Amazingly enough, with a little filtering and reverb, you can generate some very useful sounds.

Sickness or creativity? You decide! Yes, the Sonar tape simulator can serve up a nasty helping of noise.

Cakewalk's Amp Sim Effect

Here's another plug-in that doesn't get enough respect. Supposedly, this effect is for guitars. But clone a drum track, apply the Amp Sim to the clone, choose the "British Crunch" amp model, turn the "Drive" control way up, and adjust "Level" to suit. Crunchy!

Using the Fxpansion Vocoder With Sonar

I use Fxpansion's Robotik Vocoder plug-in a lot, but unlike most plug-ins, a vocoder needs two separate inputs—one for the carrier and one for the modulator. The plug-in offers two solutions: For DirectX systems, you can insert it as a bus effect; the left channel provides one input, while the right provides the other. But thanks to the VST Adapter, there's a far more desirable solution as you can run the Vocoder as a VST effect, which offers more options. Insert the Vocoder in the FX slot of the track that will serve as the carrier, while a separate plug-in called ExtModulator inserts into the FX slot of the track you want to use as a modulator.

Make sure you load both of these by right-clicking in the FX slot and following the *Audio Effects > VST* path; don't load either one as a DX effect, or the concept won't work. Load the Vocoder first, and upon loading the ExtModulator, the Vocoder's Ext. Modulation indicator will glow yellow to show it's properly connected to the ExtModulator plug-in.

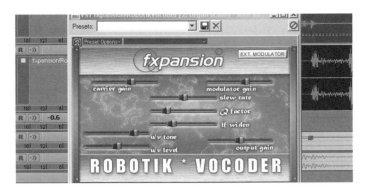

If Ext. Modulation on the Robotik Vocoder is lit, then the plug-in is recognizing the track you select-ed to serve as the modulator. In this example, track 1 is the modulator, and track 2 is the carrier. Track 2 is soloed because the vocoded loop is about to be exported as a WAV file, and you don't necessarily want the modulator to be part of the final sound.

Once everything's plugged in, trim the modulator's volume if you don't want it to be part of the overall sound (ExtModulator picks up the pre-fader signal). But if you want to export something like a vocoded loop to audio, mat-

ters get a little more complicated. Both channels *must* be selected, and so
the carrier. If the modulator channel is not selected, it won't be part of th
mixdown, so there will be no vocoder effect (and no signal, either).

One more fine point: If you save this setup as part of a file and then open it,
the vocoder will not recognize the external modulator, as it must be inserted
in the FX slot *after* inserting the vocoder. Therefore, delete ExtModulator,
then re-insert it by right-clicking on the FX slot and selecting ExtModulator
from the list of VST audio effects.

Sonitus: fx Multiband as Loudness Maximizer

Loudness maximization lets you increase a track's apparent level, and using a
multiband compressor allows you to do this fairly transparently. What's more,
the Sonitus:fx Multiband makes the process easy. To do this:

1. Insert the Sonitus fx: Multiband into a track or bus FX slot.
2. Load the multiband's Default preset. This insures that the threshold for
   each track is at maximum. We're not going to use the Multiband's compression feature, but its limiting option.
3. Go to the Multiband's "Common" tab and click on "Limit." It should glow
   yellow.
4. Add the desired amount of maximization by increasing the associated
   track's "Trim" control (which precedes the Multiband effect) rather than
   "Volume," which follows the effect.

Increasing the Trim pushes more level into the Multiband, which brings the
limiting into play. The higher the Trim level, the greater the apparent level;
but note that there is a point of diminishing returns, where the dynamics
sound squashed and unnatural.

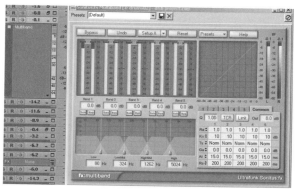

The Sonitus:fx Multiband can be put into a limiting mode that can maximize the levels of tracks,
without noticeable distortion.

creasing the trim by 3 to 6 dB seems like a good compromise between increased loudness, dynamic range, and lack of distortion, but experiment. In any event, the sound will definitely be louder. Just remember—use this power only for good! Music without significant dynamic range sounds impressive at first, but becomes aggravating after a while.

Timeworks CompressorX as Loudness Maximizer

This is a tip for those procrastinators who haven't yet made the transition from Sonar 2 to Sonar 3. Sonar 2 includes TimeWorks' CompressorX, a plug-in compressor that also offers a "brickwall," level maximization mode. As with all devices of this type, exercise restraint—particularly because the controls can be somewhat touchy. Here's how to brickwall your sound.

Here the compressor is set up more like a level maximizer. If "wall" is enabled and set to a maximum level of 0.1 dB, no signal will exceed 0.1 dB. Turning up the CompressorX "In" control causes the compressor to increase the average level, making for a "hotter" sound.

1. Insert the CompressorX into a track or bus FX slot.
2. Set the "Threshold" parameter to 0. This takes the compressor section out of the signal chain, so you needn't concern yourself with the "Attack," "Release," "Knee," or "Ratio" controls.
3. Leave "In(put)" at 0.0 for now.
4. Set the "Wall" parameter to -0.1. This allows a maximum level just under 0 (if a signal hits 0 too often in a file that's destined for CD, it may be rejected on the assumption that the 0 indications are due to overloads). Double-click on the field and type in the value, or click-shift/drag for fine-tuning.
5. Enable the Wall's "In" button toward the bottom of the plug-in.
6. The meter mode isn't crucial; I usually set it to "GR" (gain reduction) but anything other than "Off" is okay.

• Plug-Ins •

7. Increase the CompressorX's "In" control until you hear the signal hit the desired amount of loudness (typically an "In" setting of 3 - 6 dB). The average sound will become louder, but because the Wall function is in, the signal doesn't clip the channel level meters as it's clamped to the -0.1 threshold. (Of course, past a certain point, the compressor itself will start distorting internally, even if the channel doesn't distort—be careful.)

Better Vocals Through Pitch Shifting

Here's a quick tip for thickening/doubling vocals. This uses the old Cakewalk Pitch Shifter effect, which is available on the Sonar distribution CD-ROM, but is not installed as a default effect because it has been superceded by a newer time/pitch stretching processor. However, the latter is available only by selecting a Clip and going *Process > Audio Effects;* it doesn't work as a plug-in. Besides, the old one has two useful extra parameters, "Delay Time" and "Mod Depth." The quality isn't as good as the newer shifter, but it's good enough when used for a background voice—which is what we're going to do here.

First, if the Pitch Shifter isn't already present on your system, install it from the CD-ROM, as described in this chapter under "Installing Legacy Plug-Ins." Then...

1. Select the vocal track you want to thicken.
2. Go *Track > Clone.* Check "Events," "Properties," and "FX" (if it uses any FX) but do not check "Link to Original Clip." The clone needs to be independently editable.
3. Click on the Clone function "OK" button, and you now have two vocal tracks.
4. Right-click on the copied track's FX slot, and go *Audio Effects > Cakewalk > Pitch Shifter.*
5. Set the Pitch Shift parameters as follows:

• Pitch Shift = -0.24
• Dry Mix = 0
• Wet Mix = 100
• Feedback Mix = 0
• Delay Time = 2.61
• Mod Depth = 12.16

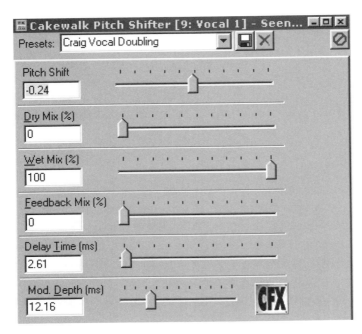

The Pitch Shifter, although it's an older effect that has to be installed manually from the distribution CD, can be an effective tool for thickening vocals. As this is being applied to a cloned track, make sure there's no Dry Mix.

These are just suggested settings that work well with my voice, feel free to adjust for the best effect with your vocals.

For the thickest, smoothest sound, pan the two vocal tracks to center. If you pan one vocal full right and one full left, you'll hear two individual vocals instead of a rich, composite vocal. Panning to opposites works very well for processing something like a background vocal chorus, as the individual parts should be thick enough by themselves; shifting pitch widens the stereo spread.

Also try panning lead vocals slightly left and right (*e.g.,* left channel at 10 o'clock, right channel at 2 o'clock). This gives a somewhat fuller sound and a somewhat wider stereo spread, which can also be useful under some circumstances.

5

DSP

Sonar includes several DSP (digital signal processing) options. These process signals, but without the use of external plug-ins. Generally, these processes are non-destructive until they're applied to the audio. However, some, like Crossfades, remain non-destructive.

THE ART OF THE CROSSFADE

Sonar offers three different types of fade curve (linear, fast, and slow), and nine different crossfade curves. Crossfades are essential when "splicing" Clips together, as they allow for a smooth transition from one Clip to the next.

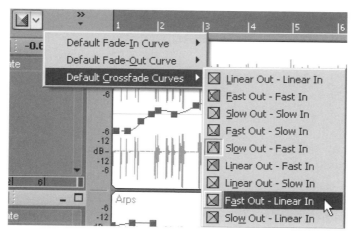

The Crossfade button is in the extreme upper left-hand corner. Next to it is the drop-down menu with the various curve options; here, the Fast Out—Linear In curve is selected.

Applying crossfades is quite painless:

1. Click on the "Crossfade" button to the immediate right of the "Snap to Grid" button.
2. Click on the little arrow to the right of the crossfade button, and a drop-down menu appears where you can choose the default fade-in, fade-out, and crossfade curve.
3. Choose the appropriate curve.
4. For a fade-out or fade-in, move the cursor to an audio Clip's upper right corner to fade out, or the upper left corner to fade in. The cursor turns into a little triangle. Click and drag to the left for a fade out, or to the right for a fade in.
5. For a crossfade, slide the two pieces of audio to be crossfaded together; a crossfade will be applied automatically to the overlapping region.

There's one caution. If you change your mind about a crossfade and slide one of the pieces of audio back so that it no longer overlaps, the crossfade curves will remain as a fade in and fade out on the two Clips that used to overlap. If this is what you want, fine. Otherwise, use the "Undo" command to return to the status prior to sliding the two pieces of audio together.

REMOVING CLICKS WHEN CONNECTING CLIPS

Some Sonar users have complained that when they try to place two differ-ent Clips end-to-end, there's a small, disturbing sound (click) on the border between them. Fortunately, it's easy to eliminate this if you know how.

A click occurs when there is an abrupt level change between two audio Clips. One cause could be DC *offset,* where a Clip's "zero-crossing" line (i.e., the place in the waveform that transitions between positive and negative) is not really zero, but higher or lower due to the offset. Unfortunately, Sonar's Audio Menu does not have a "remove DC offset" option, so you will need to export the Clip to a digital audio editor with this function (*e.g.,* Wavelab, Sound Forge, etc.). Go to the *Tools* menu; selecting your waveform editor will launch it (while leaving Sonar open) and load the Clip simultaneously.

A level change could also occur if you split or slip-edit a Clip. When slip edit-ing or splitting to a grid, the odds are remote that the snap point will occur *exactly* on a zero-crossing. To get around this, you can snap the Clip to the grid and line up the edit or slip point where you want it, but then change to the finest possible snap resolution so you can tweak the Clip start or stop to land on a zero-crossing point.

To do this, click on the small arrow next to the "Snap to Grid" button. When the Snap to Grid dialog box occurs, check "Absolute Time" and set the value to "1 sample." (This is a "sticky" setting that remains as set until changed, so change it back to your usual choice when you're done.) Then, check "Snap to Audio Zero Crossings." Move the slip edit (or split) point to the nearest zero crossing.

If this doesn't solve the problem, enable "Automatic Crossfade" (the button next to the "Snap to Grid" button). Clicking on the arrow next to the button lets you choose the default crossfade curve; I recommend "Slow Out—Fast In."

Now arrange your Clips end-to-end as desired. If there's a click, extend the end of one Clip into the beginning of the next, or vice-versa over about 2 to 4 ms (around 100 to 200 samples if you're using the "samples" time ruler calibrations).

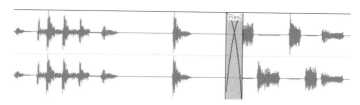

Clicking the Automatic Crossfade button causes a crossfade to occur when overlapping pieces of audio on the same track. Although there are many crossfade curve options, "Slow Out—Fast In" is a common choice for eliminating clicks; "Fast Out—Slow In" can be appropriate with more extreme click problems.

This technique works only if there is extra material beyond where the Clips begin and end (*i.e.,* you used slip-editing to create the beginning or end). If not, there will be nothing to crossfade into. This technique also doesn't work if there's a gap between Clips.

Which brings us to our final, fail-safe option: Add a very short decay time to the end of the first Clip and/or attack time at the beginning of the next Clip. Try just decay and just attack to see if either solves the problem by itself; otherwise, do both. A one to three ms fade should do the job. You can select a default fade-in and fade-out curve as well as a default crossfade curve; I generally use "Fast Curve" for the fade-out, and "Slow Curve" for the fade-in.

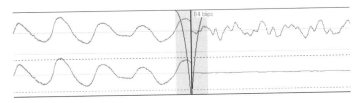

It's clear that there is a major DC level offset between these two Clips. When all else fails for getting rid of a click at the transition of one Clip to another, add a very short decay at the end of one Clip and a very short attack at the beginning of the subsequent Clip. Note that if the decay and attack times are too long, there may be an audible gap.

Here's one more tip. Before assuming you need to try one of the above procedures, first check the channel and bus meters to make sure the wave isn't going "into the red." An overload condition can generate a click.

THE MAGIC OF BOUNCE TO CLIP

One of a DAW's most useful features is the ability to cut an audio Clip into pieces, then apply selective processing—fades to eliminate clicks (see above), normalize sections that are too low in level, and so on. However, you eventually end up with a bunch of disconnected Clips that are hard to handle as a group.

The solution is the "Bounce to Clip" option, which combines the track's bits into one Clip, including the effects of any processing you've done to the Clips (however, note that automation-based changes are not applied; these still affect the Clip during real time playback). There are two ways to bounce.

Selecting Clips You Want to Bounce

The first method is to Ctrl-click on the Clips you want to bounce. Right-click on any of the selected Clips, then choose "Bounce to Clip(s)." There is a fine point: If you select non-consecutive Clips, they will be bounced together so that the Clip starts at the start of the left-most Clip you selected, and ends at the end of the right-most Clip you selected. Non-selected Clips in between are represented by silence, but they remain on the track along with the bounced Clip.

Bouncing All Clips in a Track

However, bouncing a selection of Clips is not that common a scenario. You will likely be bouncing consecutive Clips, or all the Clips in a track. So, this method involves bouncing *all* track Clips into a single track. To do this, first click on a blank space anywhere in the Clips Pane to make sure that no Clips are selected. In the Tracks Pane, click on the track number (its background turns blue) containing those Clips you want to combine. Go *Edit > Bounce to Clip(s)*...done!

APPLYING AUDIO EFFECTS

All plug-ins suck CPU power, because they're operating on a track in real time, and the CPU has to calculate the effect on playback. To reclaim some of that power, you can *apply* audio plug-in effects to a Clip, which permanently processes the effect with the particular plug-in. Once the processing is "embedded" in the audio file, you can then remove the plug-in.

To apply an effect, select the Clip(s) you want to modify, then go *Process > Apply Audio Effects*. But there are a few cautions.

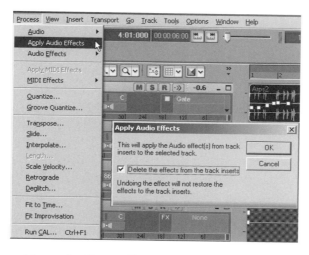

The default when applying audio effects to Clips is to delete the effects from the track inserts after any processing is complete. But unless you're really sure that the effect is perfect and you're not going to want to tweak it later, uncheck this box and delete the effect manually only after you're sure everything is as you want it, or you need to reclaim CPU power.

Applying audio effects works on selected Clips, not an entire track. To process all the Clips in a track, select all of them.

If you apply processing to a Groove Clip, it will lose its groove properties and revert to being a regular Clip. Had you painstakingly set your markers for the perfect "acidization," you'll have to start over if you decide to, for example, add a little limiting. (I tried doing the editing in Wavelab instead, but it too destroys Groove Clip marker positions.) However, there is a solution: Adobe Audition *does* retain the groove markers after processing, even if you change the bit depth. If you're into developing loops, it might be worth buying a copy just for its ability to edit and save Groove Clips while retaining the groove markers.

Groove Clip data will be retained if you use the *Process > Audio Effects* function to add an effect to the Clip, instead of using *Process > Apply Audio Effects* to apply the effect inserted in the FX slot to a Clip.

TO DITHER OR NOT TO DITHER?

Dithering is another example of DSP; its main purpose is to maintain audio quality while going from higher-resolution to lower-resolution audio formats.

For example, Sonar can record and playback with either 16- or 24-bit audio resolution. For a given sample rate, 24-bit resolution takes up 50% more disk space than 16-bit resolution, but for some projects (*e.g.,* acoustic music) the fidelity is worth it. On the other hand, if you're going to compress the living daylights out of a dance mix, 24 bits is probably not worth the extra space.

Assuming you use 24-bit operation, what happens to the "extra" eight bits when your music ends up on a 16-bit/44.1 kHz CD? Before the advent of dithering, they were simply discarded (just imagine how those poor bits felt, especially after being called the "least significant bits" all their lives). If you've heard a "buzzing" sort of sound at the end of a fade out or reverb tail with 16-bit resolution, that's because the least significant bit, which tries to follow the audio signal, switches back and forth rapidly between 0 and 1. In a 24-bit recording, there are 256 different possible levels (the lower 8 bits) between that "on" and "off" condition, but once the recording has been truncated, the resolution is no longer there to reproduce those changes. This buzzing is called *quantization* noise, because the noise occurs during the process of quantizing the audio into discrete steps.

Dithering adds random noise to the lowest eight bits of the 24-bit signal. This noise is different for the two channels in order not to degrade stereo separation. Therefore, the lowest part of the dynamic range no longer correlates directly to the original signal, but to a combination of the noise source and information present in the lowest eight bits. This reduces the quantization noise, providing in its place a smoother type of hiss modulated by the lower-level information. The most obvious audible benefit is that fades become smoother and more realistic, but there's also more sonic detail.

Sonar can dither 24-bit signals down to 16 bits. You can enable or disable dithering in two different places: Under *Options* > *Audio* > "Advanced" tab, check or uncheck "Apply Dither." Under *Tools* > *Change Audio Format,* if you select 16 bits, the dither box is enabled.

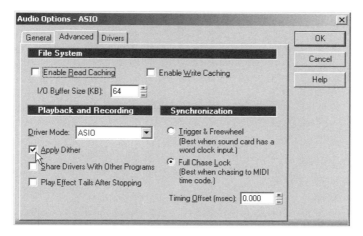

Applying dither in Sonar is simply a matter of checking the dither option. Unlike most digital audio editors, you do not have a choice of dithering algorithms, or type of noiseshaping.

However, I recommend that you usually leave dither unchecked. The dithering used in Sonar is designed to make 16-bit files sound a little better, but adds processing time. It can also slow down real-time effects performance with slower computers. But perhaps more importantly, the cardinal rule of dithering is that you should not re-dither material that has already been dithered. Therefore, dithering is invariably performed as the very last step of the mastering process. Let's consider various scenarios, and assume the delivery medium is a standard CD.

You record with 24-bit resolution: At some point, your recording will need to lose 8 bits. If you use a digital audio editor like Wavelab, Sound Forge, Adobe Audition, etc. it's best to export Sonar's file as a 24-bit file, import the 24-bit file into your digital audio editor, do whatever mastering operations are required, then use the editor's dithering algorithm to create the final 16-bit master. You will likely have a choice of dithering algorithms and maybe even noise shaping characteristics (*i.e.,* methods of shifting any noise to less audible portions of the audio spectrum), as opposed to Sonar's lone dithering choice.

You record with 16-bit resolution without dithering: Do the same as above. Even though the exported file and the final file will be 16 bits, if you do any editing with the digital audio editor, any processing will almost certainly exploit the editor's higher internal resolution, thereby increasing the word length of the original 16-bit file. Apply dithering within the editing program when you save the final version of the file.

You record with 16 or 24-bit resolution but had dithering enabled:
Import the file into your digital audio editor, do any required editing, but do not add dithering when you export the final file. Because the material was already dithered, the digital audio editing program should retain that dithering.

You record with 24-bit resolution and want to export from Sonar directly to the final mastered version: This is a situation where you want to enable dithering in the "Audio Options" dialog.

Here's one final caution: If you plan to crossfade tracks on your CD, make sure neither file is dithered. Crossfading the dithered sections could lead to artifacts; you're better off crossfading the two, then dithering the combination.

SONAR'S VOCAL HARMONY GENERATOR

Have you used Sonar's intelligent harmony generator function? Probably not, because it doesn't exist. But if you're willing to provide the intelligence (*i.e.,* teach Sonar the rules of harmony), Sonar will provide the harmonization. Here's how.

First, create two clones from your original vocal (right-click on the vocal track number and select "Clone Track," then repeat for the second track). One will provide the Major 3rd harmony and the other will provide the Minor 3rd.

Sonar has a Time/Pitch Stretch DSP processor (not a plug-in) that can synthesize a harmony part from your original vocal. There are two ways to apply it to a Clip or Track:

1. Select the Clip(s) or Track you want to process.
2. Right-click on the Clip(s), and go *Audio Effects > Cakewalk > Time/Pitch Stretch*. Or, don't right-click and instead go *Process > Audio Effects > Cakewalk > Time/Pitch Stretch*.
3. When the Time/Pitch Stretch dialog box appears, proceed with editing its parameters.

• DSP •

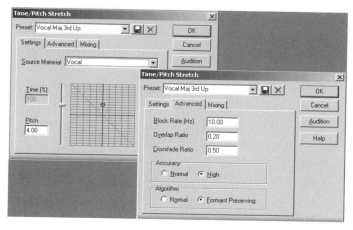

The Time/Pitch Stretch processor works very well with vocals, assuming you set the parameters correctly. There are presets for Vocal Maj 3rd Up and Vocal 3rd Up (minor third); this picture shows recommended parameter values for the "Settings" and "Advanced" tabs.

The Time/Pitch Stretch module has three tabs, "Settings," "Advanced," and "Mixing." For mixing, specify whether you want the output result to be stereo or mono. Generally, you'll specify the same result as the original track (*i.e.,* stereo result for a stereo track).

You can save some time by calling up the preset "Vocal Maj 3rd Up" for major harmonies, which sets "Pitch" to +4 semitones and specifies "Vocal" for the Source Material in the drop-down menu. On the "Advanced" page, make sure that "Accuracy" is set to "High," and "Algorithm" to "Formant Preserving." You can just leave "Block Rate," "Overlap Ratio," and "Crossfade Ratio" as is, or experiment with the settings if you're so inclined.

To hear the effect, click on the Audition button. Remember, though, that the audition duration may be limited to a few seconds; if the vocal Clip has a lot of dead air at the beginning, you may not hear the results of the processing. Either slip-edit the beginning of the Clip, or extend the audition time by going *Options > Global >* "General" tab, and changing the "Audition Commands For" parameter. Note that longer audition times will require more processing before you can hear the effect in action.

So to recap, we have the original vocal, one track transposed up a Major 3rd, and one track transposed up a Minor 3rd. The next step is to cut out those phrases from the harmonies that aren't compatible with the original vocal. For example, if one part requires a major harmony, remove the matching phrase from the minor harmony, and vice-versa.

This requires a lot of cutting, but you're going to have to do it anyway, because the Time/Pitch Stretch doesn't preserve length perfectly—the tracks I've processed always stretch a little bit long, requiring cutting bits from the harmony lines and lining them up with the main vocal. Although it might appear there's an easy fix for this—just shorten the time using the Pitch/Stretch's time-stretching function—this can't be accessed if "Formant Preservation" is on. And if you turn off "Formant Preservation," then the sound quality for vocals is nowhere near as good. You can make the vocal an exact number of measures and convert it into a Groove Clip, but that really messes with the stretched sound.

Not surprisingly, real harmonies from a human singer will usually sound better. But synthesizing harmonies creates a distinctive timbre that may be desirable for some songs; in fact, sometimes you might not want to use formant preservation to get a more whacked-out effect.

TIME FOR A TUNE UP

This DSP doesn't modify anything, but monitors tuning. You can access Sonar's built-in tuner by going *Tools > Tuner*. To use it, check which track is being fed by the instrument you want to tune, then make it the active track. The tuner will then read the sound card input to that track (identified in the tuner's title bar).

The help file says that you need to disarm all tracks prior to using the tuner, but I didn't find this to be true; the active track can be record-enabled and the tuner will work just fine. (I also noticed other tracks can be record-enabled too. As long as the track you want to tune is the active track, everything seems to work out okay.) Although the track's meter will not register, the meter on the bottom of the tuner will advise you of the incoming signal strength. Note that the tuner likes a fairly strong signal.

The tuner shows the deviation in cents along the top, the note name, and arrows to indicate whether the pitch is sharp, flat, or on pitch. The lower meter indicates signal strength. Okay, so a tuner isn't exactly the most ground-breaking concept, but it's one of those thoughtful little extras that helps save time.

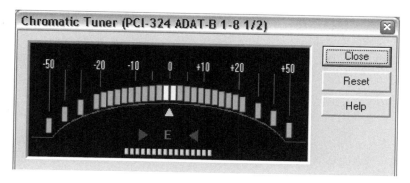

Sonar's tuner is very handy for quick tuning touch-ups. Here it's monitoring a channel coming in the ADAT interface of a MOTU 2408. This feeds Track 1, which is record-enabled. Note how the title bar shows the interface input being monitored, and also, that the E string is perfectly in tune.

6

AUTOMATION

AUTOMATION BASICS

Automation provides the ability to record changes in parameters such as level, panning, and send controls for mixer channels (tracks), as well as parameters for virtual instruments (DXi and VST), VST effects, and some DirectX-compatible effects providing the manufacturer included the proper "hooks" in their software to allow automation control.

Track automation allows changing the mix dynamically; virtual instrument automation lets you create effects like dramatic filter sweeps, change vibrato rate, and the like. Effects automation can help add interest to a song—for example, try dropping the guitar EQ a bit in the midrange when the singer comes in, and boosting it during the solo. The effect of making the guitar less or more prominent via EQ can be more interesting than just doing volume changes.

Sonar has three main ways to add automation:

1. Record control movements that you make on-screen. This works for all track automation, and for some virtual instrument and soft synths. Recording these movements creates envelopes within tracks in the Clips Pane, which you can then edit if desired.
2. Record automation data from an external hardware control unit optimized to work with Sonar. This works the same way as recording on-screen control movements, except that the hardware sends messages to Sonar, which it then interprets as automation data.
3. Record MIDI controller messages from an external control unit, which create MIDI controller envelopes. These then control parameters within MIDI-compatible devices, such as virtual instruments and some effects.

4. Draw track automation envelopes or MIDI controllers directly in the track. This is a non-real time process and is ideal for when you want to add automation that is too complex to do using the other three methods.

DX AND VST PROCESSOR AUTOMATION

Many of the DirectX effects included with Sonar include automatable parameters, but automatable parameters in suitable VST effects are also useable in Sonar thanks to the VST Adapter utility, which has been built in to Sonar starting with V3.

Of the four automation options mentioned above, the one you'll use depends on which method the manufacturer implemented in the plug-in (capture real-time control changes, or non-real-time creation of automation envelopes). It's also possible in some cases to combine the two options, and record some envelopes in real time, but draw in others.

Recording Real-Time Automation Moves with Effects

1. If a processor is not already inserted, right-click on the FX slot, and select the desired processor.
2. Right-click on the processor name and select Arm Parameter (if that option is grayed out, then there are no automatable parameters).
3. A dialog box listing the automatable parameters appears. Check the parameters for which you want to record automation, then click on "OK" to close the box. You're now prepared to do automation.
4. To record the moves, click on the Record Automation button in the Transport toolbar. If it's grayed out, that means either one or more tracks are in the standard record mode, which must be turned off prior to recording automation; or no parameters are selected for automation.
5. As soon as you click on the Record Automation button, it turns red, and the Transport starts playing. Move the controls that correspond to the parameters being automated. When you stop the Transport, your automation edits will have been recorded.
6. Play back, and the knobs will move to follow the envelopes (I must say moving knobs are a never-ending source of fascination to clients, and I highly recommend having lots of knobs moving around on-screen if you plan to raise your rates in the near future).

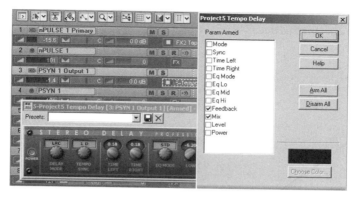

Enable the automation parameters you want to record, click on the "Record Automation" button in the Transport toolbar, then tweak the controls in real time. Editable envelopes will appear in the Clips Pane after recording; nodes can snap to grid markings, which is very convenient when creating rhythmically-related effects. In this example, the Tempo Delay processor from Cakewalk's Project5 is having its "Feedback" and "Mix" parameters selected for automation.

Once the envelopes are there, you can edit them as you would any automation envelopes—delete or add nodes, and raise and lower entire envelopes.

You can even reassign an envelope to a different parameter: Right-click on the envelope line itself, select "Assign Envelope," and check the envelope to which the current envelope should be reassigned.

Recording Effects Automation Envelopes in Non-Real Time

The envelope method of automation is equally straightforward.

The process of enabling non-real-time envelope drawing is similar to the real-time control method. However, as these envelopes are associated with the track, you access them by right-clicking on the track. In this picture, parameters from IK Multimedia's AmpliTube are about to be selected for automation.

1. Right-click on the track (not an envelope) containing the effect.
2. Select "Envelopes."
3. Choose the "Create Track Envelope" option. This brings forth a menu that shows any "standard" envelopes (aux send, pan, etc.), as well as another option for the effect itself.

When you choose the effect, a check box similar to the one for real time automation appears. This time, checking a box means that an envelope corresponding to that parameter will appear in the track. These start off as straight lines, but can be manipulated into any shape you want.

HIDING AND MANAGING AUTOMATION ENVELOPES

As you might expect, if you end up doing track automation and lots of effects automation, the track can become pretty cluttered with nodes and lines for all the envelopes. To deal with this:

1. Right-click on the track.
2. Go *Envelopes* > *Show Track Envelopes.*
3. Uncheck any envelopes you don't want to see (they still affect the sound, of course). You can always re-enable them again later. Or, hide an envelope by right-clicking on the envelope line itself, and selecting "Hide Envelope." This automatically unchecks the box under Show Track Envelopes.

For envelope management on a grander scale, click on the "Envelope Tool" button, and you'll see a list of possibilities for turning various combinations of envelopes on and off. For example, if you plan to do any intensive audio editing, it's helpful to select "Hide All Envelopes" to minimize distractions.

The envelope tool makes it easy to hide and show groups of envelopes, or all envelopes. Just click on the downward arrow to the right of the Scrub button.

SOFT SYNTH AUTOMATION: THE FINE PRINT

Some people have trouble automating soft synth parameters because it appears that knob motions aren't being recorded. However, not all soft synths work identically. Some can record control motion; others respond only to automation via envelopes. Some accommodate both methods.

Automating with Controller Movements

For example, here's how to automate the DreamStation synth (included with Sonar) using MIDI controllers—you don't even need to click on the "Automation" button.

1. Go *Insert > DXi Synth > DreamStation DXi2.*
2. When the "Insert DXi Synth Options" appears, make sure the following boxes are checked: "MIDI Source Track," "First Synth Output (Audio)," and "Synth Property Page."
3. Click on "OK" to insert the instrument into the synth rack.
4. This process creates a MIDI track whose data will play the DreamStation, and an audio track for its audio output. You should also see the DreamStation's front panel because you checked the "Synth Property Page" box. (If the front panel doesn't appear, double-click on the corresponding audio track's "Input" field).
5. Select the corresponding MIDI track by clicking on the track number.
6. Arm the track for recording by clicking on the track's "R" button.
7. Begin recording (click on the Transport's Record button, or type "R"), and start moving some of the knobs with your mouse.
8. Click on "Stop." You'll see controller data recorded in the track's Clips Pane.
9. On playback, the DreamStation knobs will move to follow what you recorded.

Automating with Envelopes

If you prefer to use envelopes with the example above:

1. Right-click (in the Clips Pane) on an empty space in the MIDI track driving the DreamStation.
2. Go *Envelopes > Create Track Envelopes > MIDI.*
3. The drop-down menu under "Value" shows the DreamStation's automatable parameters. For example, select "Controller 37—Filter Cutoff," then click on "OK."

4. An envelope will appear in the track, which you can then edit.
5. On playback, this envelope will move the "Filter Cutoff" control.

Differences with DXi and VSTi Instrument Automation

Now let's consider Native Instrument's DXi version of the FM7 soft synth. Unlike automatable effects, DXi devices do not provide for the standard "Arm Parameter" dialog box. So, there's no way to arm parameters, and if you move parameter sliders, Sonar will not record their motion. However, you can automate the FM7 parameters via envelopes, and its knobs will respond on playback. Furthermore, for hands-on control, use an external fader box (or suitable wheels, data sliders, etc. on a keyboard) and assign MIDI controller numbers to the FM7 parameters you want to control. Record the fader movement into Sonar as MIDI data, and on playback, the knob will follow this data.

Case closed? Not quite. If you use a VST-based instrument with Cakewalk's VST Adapter, the automation landscape changes yet again as you *can* use the Arm Parameter option. However, this requires inserting an instrument manually, not using the synth rack. This works as follows:

1. Create an audio track by right-clicking on an empty spot in the Tracks Pane and selecting "Insert Audio Track."
2. Right-click in the FX slot and go *DXi Synth > [name of synth you want to insert]*.
3. Right-click on the instrument name in the FX slot, and select "Arm Parameter."
4. As the instrument probably wasn't designed to be used this way, the list of parameters may show each parameter neatly with its name, a bunch of MIDI continuous controllers, or at worst, gibberish. Proceed as you would when using the "Arm Parameter" option with effects.

When you don't use the synth rack, you will also need to create a MIDI track to drive the instrument, and send its output to the instrument (click the arrow in the MIDI track's output field, and select the desired instrument).

Remember, extensive automation stresses any program, so save frequently.

TYPICAL AUTOMATION RESULTS

A "wrapper" like Cakewalk's VST Adapter doesn't have to work very hard to play notes, but the real test comes with automation. The table below shows the results for automating several instruments using VST Adapter. I also tried using another wrapper, DirectiXer, that's not made by Cakewalk; it didn't work as well with the soft synths, but does offer the ability to record control motions for *some* VST instruments into MIDI tracks as MIDI Non-Registered Parameter Numbers (NRPNs).

Here's what each column heading stands for:

Format: Either DXi (Sonar's preferred format) or VSTi.

ArmP (Arm Parameter): "Y" (yes) means you can load the instrument into the FX bin, right-click, and choose the controls whose motion you want to record in real time.

Menv (MIDI Track Envelope): If "Y," you can right-click in the instrument's MIDI control track, and create envelopes to control parameters.

Aenv (Audio Track Envelope): This works with instruments where you can arm parameters. "Y" means you can right-click in the instrument's audio track and create envelopes that modify particular parameters. Note that as you drag the envelope, the controlled parameter's knob, switch, etc. will follow the envelope value. An existing envelope will be overwritten if you Arm Parameter and do new control motions.

Mrec (MIDI Recording): If "Y," you can manipulate knobs on the instrument, and the motions will be recorded in the instrument's associated MIDI track.

XMC (External MIDI Control): If "Y," then you can feed in external MIDI control signals that manipulate the instrument parameters, which can also be recorded in the instrument's MIDI track to provide automation.

Also see the notes below the chart.

Instrument	Format	ArmP	Menv	Aenv	Mrec	XMC
DreamStation DXi2	DXi	N	Y	N	Y	Y
Edirol VSC	DXi	N	Y	N	Y	Y
Emagic EVP73	VST	Y	Y	Y	N	N(1)
Fxpansion DR-008	DXi	N	Y	N	N	Y
Green Oak Crystal	VST	Y(2)	Y(3)	N	N	Y(3)
NI B4	DXi	N	Y	N	N	Y
NI B4	VST	Y	Y	Y	N	Y
NI Battery	DXi	N	Y	N	N	Y
NI Battery	VST	Y	Y	Y	N	Y
NI FM7	DXi	N	Y	N	N	Y
NI FM7	VST	Y	Y	Y	N	Y
NI Kontakt	DXi	N	Y	N	N	Y
NI Kontakt	VST	N(4)	Y	N	N	Y
NI Pro-53	DXi	N	Y	N	N	Y
NI Pro-53	VST	Y	Y	Y	N	Y

Instrument	Format	ArmP	Menv	Aenv	Mrec	XMC
ReValver SE	DXi	N	Y	N	N	N
Rgc Audio Triangle II	DXi	N	Y	N	N	Y
Steinberg HALion	VST	N(5)	Y	N	N	Y
Steinberg LM4 MII (6)	VST	Y	Y	Y	N	N
Steinberg Model-E	VST	Y(7)	Y	N	N	Y
Steinberg Neon	VST	Y	Y	Y	N	Y
Steinberg Plex	VST	Y	Y	Y	N	Y

1. This should have worked with MIDI controllers, but seemed to work only with NRPN automation.
2. No parameters showed up, but checking "select all" allowed choosing and programming them.
3. Parameter values follow the envelopes, but controls don't reflect these changes (although they change colors to show they've been tied to external control).
4. No parameters showed up in the Arm Parameter check list, and checking "Select All" didn't choose them.
5. A list of parameters appears, but doesn't work for parameter automation, and envelopes can't be created in the audio track. MIDI controller-based automation works, however.
6. Generally slow graphic response—you get the feeling it's working hard to do automation, even though the sound is okay.
7. Often glitches when moving parameters while recording, but this problem doesn't occur on playback.

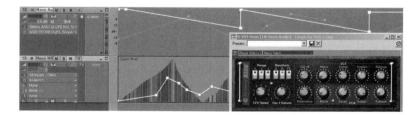

It may be old and basic, but Steinberg's Neon works like a champ with Sonar thanks to the VST Adapter. Here, two envelopes for parameter control have been added in the Audio track, two more in the MIDI track, and also, a MIDI controller curve has been recorded from a MIDI fader box's output.

As is clear from the chart, different instruments respond in different ways to automation. Some methods work better than others, although this is partially a matter of choice. Personally, I'd rather use a fader box than a mouse for control. Of course, those who aren't as much into real-time control might prefer using envelopes.

"CROSS-CONTROLLING" INSTRUMENTS

Here's a fine point about DXi automation via MIDI. Sonar defaults to bouncing DXi MIDI data to the MIDI track whose output is assigned to the DXi. If you want to record MIDI control changes, assign the track's MIDI out to the DXi you want to control.

However, you can also record DXi knob motion on any MIDI track (assuming, of course, that the DXi can generate MIDI data). Go *Options > Global >* "MIDI" tab and check "Echo DXi Input to All MIDI Tracks."

One DreamStation is assigned to track 2, the other to track 3. Each has a different patch loaded, but changing the filter cutoff on the first DreamStation instance changes the same parameter identically on the second DreamStation.

Why would you want to do this? If you don't have a hardware fader box, you can use the controllers on an instrument like the DreamStation to control parameters in other instruments or effects.

Echoing to all tracks is also useful if you open multiple instances of an instrument and want a "master" control. For example, in one tune I had two DreamStations opened and panned oppositely, each with a different bass sound. But I also wanted their filters to open and close in tandem. I could have recorded the changes for one and pasted the data, but it was easier to record-enable the MIDI tracks driving each instance, and move the control. That way I could also hear, in real-time, how this affected the sound of both devices playing together.

RE-DISCOVERING SNAPSHOT AUTOMATION

Fader automation is so ubiquitous that it's easy to overlook the less glamorous, but highly useful, snapshot automation. This type of automation gets its name because it is not a dynamic process, but rather, captures the parameter settings at a particular Now Time. There are two snapshot automation techniques: Per-parameter, and multiple parameters (interestingly, the online help describes only the multiple parameter process).

The per-parameter snapshot places a node on the corresponding automation envelope if such an envelope exists. If not, it creates the envelope and places a node. To take a snapshot of an individual parameter, place the Now Time where you want to enter the automation event for a particular parameter. Then, adjust the parameter (e.g., level, pan, EQ frequency, send amount, etc.) to the desired value. Right-click on the parameter control, and choose Automation Snapshot.

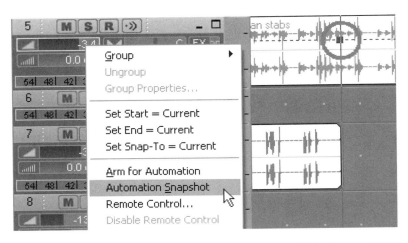

A right-click on the fader in the upper left has brought up a menu with the Automation Snapshot option. Selecting this has dropped an automation node in the related track (circled for clarity).

The procedure for creating a snapshot that encompasses multiple parameters is a little more complex. You would use this if you want, for example, several tracks to change volume instantly and at the same place, such as when switching from intro to verse.

If the Automation toolbar isn't visible, go *View > Toolbars* and check "Automation." Next, place the Now Time where you want to place the automation events, and arm automation for each parameter that you want to include in the snapshot (right-click on the parameter and choose "Arm for Automation").

Adjust each parameter value as desired. To enter these parameter values as automation, click on the Automation toolbar's "Camera" ("snapshot") button. Do *not* click on the "Record Automation" button—we don't want the transport to play. Entering snapshots can occur only when the transport is stopped.

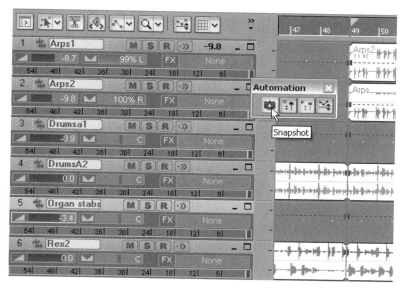

The level controls in the tracks have all been armed for automation. Clicking on the Snapshot button in the Automation toolbar places a node in each track's level envelope, at the Now Time.

To disarm all the armed tracks after you're done taking the snapshot, click the button to the right of the snapshot button in the Automation toolbar. (The next button to the right enables/disables automation playback.)

7

CONTROL SURFACES

Many people (certainly including me!) feel that a good mix can be just as much a "performance" as playing live, and that part of the fun of mixing is spontaneously moving faders as the spirit moves you. Automation using envelopes and on-screen faders often minimizes this type of interaction, as many engineers have a tendency to automate in small chunks, punching in new moves as needed. Besides with a mouse, you can't automate more than one parameter at a time.

However, it doesn't have to be this way. A good control surface can restore real-time control using some combination of faders, knobs, and switches. Then, if you enable automation, you'll be able to store the results of your mixing performance—giving the best of both worlds.

We'll start with the simplest possible control method: Using MIDI to control Key Bindings.

REMOTE CONTROL USING MIDI KEY BINDINGS

Sonar has extensive keyboard shortcut options, but you can also use MIDI keys as shortcuts (nor are the two mutually exclusive). This is particularly useful in two situations: Your MIDI controller is located some distance away from your computer so you need remote control, or you want to use something like M-Audio's Oxygen8 mini-keyboard as a control center for Sonar. (This is also a good use for old drum machines if the pads output MIDI notes.)

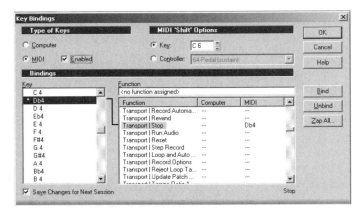

The Key Bindings menu works for computer keys or MIDI *keyboard notes. Here, Db4 is bound to the Transport Stop function. Note that the "Enabled" box must be checked for the* MIDI *key triggers to have an effect.*

Setting up MIDI control keys is pretty easy. Go *Options > Key Bindings,* and click on the "MIDI" button.

Sonar lets you designate a single keyboard note as a "Shift" key, so that you can play the keyboard normally but holding down the Shift key, then hitting another note, triggers a particular function (I use the highest note as the shift key, as I seldom hit it in normal playing). To set the Shift key, highlight the "Key" field and play the desired note. (You can also use a controller like mod wheel to enable the shift function, but I find using a key easier.)

Now "bind" a note to a specific function. Hit the key you want to use for the trigger; the key is highlighted in the left-most window. Scroll down the list in the right window to the desired function. Click on the function, then click on "Bind" (or type "Alt-B"). This creates a line from the key name to the function.

After creating a binding, a dot shows up to the left of the key name. Click on any of these dotted keys, and you'll see the function to which it is bound. Unbind a key by highlighting the key name and clicking on "Unbind," or use "Zap All" to disconnect all bindings. Note that you can enable/disable all MIDI bindings with the Enabled check box, which you'll want to do if you're play-ing a part that requires the use of the designated shift key (otherwise, Sonar will just ignore that key if you play it).

Incidentally, here are the key bindings that work for me: C = Rewind, C♯ = Stop, D = Previous Marker, D♯ = Play, E = Next Marker, F = Record, F♯ = Undo, G = Record Automation.

• Control Surfaces •

BASIC REMOTE CONTROL USING CONTROLLERS

If you don't really need a full-blown control surface, but just want some hands-on control over some crucial parameters while mixing, there's a simple solution. For this type of application, just about anything that generates MIDI data—a MIDI keyboard with mod wheel and data slider, a MIDI footpedal, or simple fader box—will do the job.

In the Tracks Pane, you can automate volume, pan, aux sends and pans, pre/post switch, phase switch, and stereo/mono switch. To set up a parameter for remote control, right-click on the parameter. If it can be remote-controlled, Remote Control will be available; select it, and the Remote Control window appears.

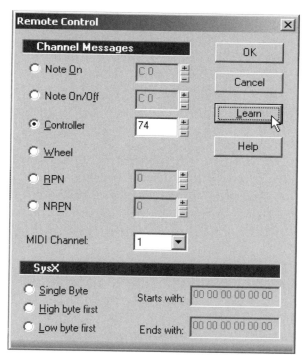

Controls can respond to a wide variety of MIDI messages, including sys ex. The Learn function is particularly handy if you're not sure what controller number a particular piece of hardware generates. Here, the Learn function has shown that a controller is generating MIDI controller #74.

This window is where you assign a controller to the parameter. Choose "Note On," "Note On/Off," "Controller," "Wheel," "RPN," or "NRPN." When using a controller, you can just move the controller from one extreme to another and back again, then click on "Learn." The Remote Control box will indicate the controller number.

As you vary the controller's physical knob, the associated parameter should change in tandem. You can then proceed with standard automation techniques (right-click on the parameter, select "Arm for Automation," and click on the Transport's "Automation" button). Moving the control generates a standard automation envelope.

If you group audio tracks together (*i.e.,* right-click on specific tracks and assign them to a common group), you can write parallel automation moves for all group tracks with a single control. However, each track in the group needs to have "Remote Control" enabled and set to the correct incoming controller message, and each track must also have "Arm for Automation" enabled.

TOTAL CONTROL

If you want to go for the gusto, Sonar works with a lot of commercially-available control surfaces. To get started, first you need a Sonar-compatible control surface. Well, not actually—you can program a "generic" surface, but it's a lot easier to get started with something for which there already exists a template that's been tweaked to work specifically with Sonar.

Sonar comes with one pre-installed template for the Cakewalk Generic Surface. To add a specific control surface, go *Options > Control Surfaces.* A box appears that shows all connected surfaces. To add a surface, click on the star button, and choose from TASCAM US-428, Cakewalk Generic Surface, C.M. Labs MotorMix, DigiTech RPx, Radikal Technologies SAC-2.2 or SAC-2K, MMC, Mackie Control XT, Mackie Control, or whatever else has been added in new revisions of the program.

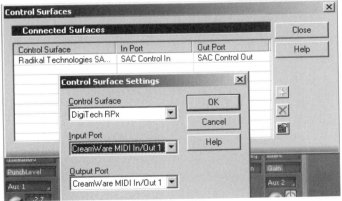

The Control Surfaces box shows connected control surfaces, and also allows adding others. In this example, the Radikal Technologies controller is connected, and the DigiTech RPx controller is about to be added to the list.

Although standard faders are useful, especially for signal processing and soft synth parameters, for mixing you really want motorized faders. Because these follow the automation moves and are almost certainly touch-sensitive, you can leave the automation enabled, and the faders will follow along with whatever automation is already recorded on the track. As soon as you grab the fader and move it, new moves overwrite old ones.

I've used Sonar with the Radikal Technologies SAC-2.2, Peavey StudioMix, and Mackie Control (which all have motorized faders), as well as the Event EZBus, which has standard faders and uses a fader nulling system. If you're not familiar with fader nulling, it's a far less expensive alternative to motorized faders but still addresses the problem that a fader's physical position may not correspond to the current automation value. With typical fader nulling schemes, two LEDs indicate whether the fader is above or below the current automation value. You then move the fader until neither LED is lit, which means the fader matches the automation value. You can then punch in automation, and write new automation moves.

The StudioMix is no longer made, but in retrospect, it was a superb combination of compact size and most of what you want a control surface to do. The Mackie Control provides value for money, while the SAC-2.2 is great for this type of thing, especially if you use both Macs and PCs in your studio—it's not only cross-platform, but can network between the two systems.

TYPICAL CONTROL SURFACE INSTALLATION

Let's look at how you'd install a control surface in Sonar. In this case, we'll use the Radikal Technologies SAC-2.2 because it offers both MIDI and USB control (although USB is the preferred option). As an example this allows us to investigate both options; use whichever is appropriate for your control surface.

1. Boot up Sonar.
2. If you've already enabled MIDI ports in Sonar, plan to the run the SAC-2.2 in MIDI mode, and it is already plugged into ports that are enabled, skip to step 5. Otherwise, continue.
3. If you have not enabled MIDI ports and plan to run the control surface in MIDI mode, enable the MIDI ports into which you plugged the surface's MIDI I/O. To do this, go *Options > MIDI Devices,* and select the appropriate MIDI in and out. If you want to use USB mode, under MIDI Devices choose "SAC Control In" under Inputs and "SAC Control Out" under Outputs. This is in addition to any other MIDI ports being used for interfacing. (In USB mode, the SAC provides another MIDI in and out port that you may want to enable and use.)

4. After choosing the MIDI Devices, click on "OK."
5. Go *Options > Control Surfaces.*
6. Click on the "Add New Control Surface" button (the button that looks like a little star).
7. From the pop-up menu, select your supported control surface in the "Control Surface" field.
8. Choose the appropriate connections for the "Input Port" and "Output Port" fields. For USB operation with the SAC-2.2, these are "SAC Control In" and "SAC Control Out" respectively. For MIDI, these are the ports into which you connected the control surface's MIDI in and out ports.
9. Click on "OK," then on "Close" to close the Control Surfaces window.
10. Go *View > Toolbars,* click on "Control Surfaces," then click on "Close." From the toolbar that appears, select the control surface you just installed. The faders should snap to attention, and you're ready to go.

Assigning Function Buttons

If your control surface has assignable function buttons, clicking on the Control Surfaces Toolbar's "Properties" button brings up a list of Function Buttons, which you can freely assign. While you're there, hit "F1" for help, which brings up comprehensive documentation on using your control surface with Sonar. With more recently added control surfaces, this information may not be included with the main online help.

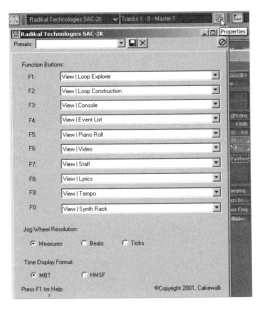

Remote control function buttons allow assigning particular functions to convenient, one-button access.

MIXING WITH CONTROLLERS

To me, the main advantage of using hardware faders is the ability to add real-time, spontaneous dynamics. I love pumping that single snare drum that hits on the offbeat just before the chorus kicks in, but there's more to dynamics than that.

Adding small rhythmic "pushes" to the level creates a more animated, lively mix. Unlike pitch discrimination, the ear isn't all that sensitive to small level changes. Thus, these small variations are "felt" rather than "heard." Although many musicians are satisfied to draw in level changes with a mouse, they'll never convince me that the mix will have the same degree of animation as one where you make on-the-fly, spontaneous decisions about which tracks should dominate or lay back further in the track.

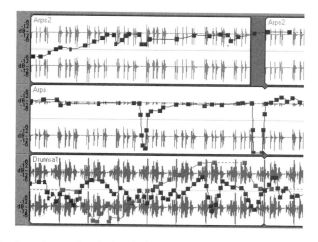

These three tracks show the results of using fader movement to add animation. It would be at least time-consuming, and at most absurdly difficult, to create these types of complex envelopes using the "click and draw" method. Note that the third track has both volume and pan automation curves.

Changing Overall Envelope Levels

However, there are two main concerns when doing these types of moves: What happens if you get the moves right, but the overall level needs to go up or down? There are two main options.

Per Clip: It's easy to change a Clip envelope's overall level (note that you can create a Clip containing the area where you want the level to change just by adding a split at the beginning and end). First, select the Clip by clicking on it (but not on any envelope superimposed on the Clip). All the envelope nodes will now be selected. Drag up or down on any node to raise or lower all of them, respectively. However, if a node is at maximum level, the envelope cannot be raised, nor can it be lowered if any node is at minimum.

Per Track: The following is the method I prefer when it's time to switch gears from making the various moves to creating the final mix. Click on the "Envelope/Offset Mode" button, and all the faders will have little (+) symbols next to them. This means that any control changes will move an entire envelope up or down in level.

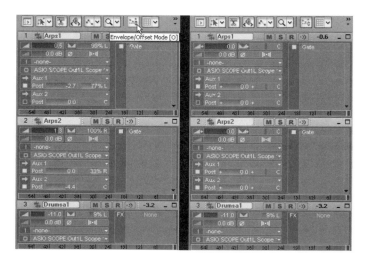

The Tracks Pane view on the left in is Envelope mode, where the fader settings reflect those of any envelopes; the cursor is about to click on the Envelope/Offset mode button. The Tracks Pane view on the right has Offset mode enabled, where the faders act like "master volume controls" for the envelope settings. Note how the "Vol," "Pan," and "Snd" controls have a small (+) next to them to remind you that Offset mode is enabled.

8

REWIRE

Sonar can work in perfect synchronization with other programs, thanks to ReWire compatibility. This doesn't just mean timing sync, although that is one of ReWire's talents, but synchronization of tracks and workflow. For example, you can use Propellerhead Softwares' Reason as a rack of virtual instruments for Sonar, and their names and outputs will show up in Sonar's mixer. Or, you can ReWire Cakewalk's Project5 into Sonar to add a wicked pattern-based sequencer and collection of synths to Sonar's repertoire. If you want to get rhythm section ideas down fast, link up ReBirth's drum and bass line modules, or Arturia's Storm, into Sonar. Ableton's Live is excellent for integrating a live performance-oriented program with Sonar.

REWIRE BASICS

Sonar serves as a ReWire host. In other words, other ReWire *clients* can insert into Sonar, but Sonar cannot insert into other ReWire-compatible hosts. For example, with a client like Reason "rewired" into Sonar, Reason's instrument outputs go into Sonar's mixer and show up as Sonar tracks. MIDI data recorded into Sonar can flow to Reason, thus allowing the various soft synths to be triggered within Sonar. Transport functions are shared, so that starting or stopping one program starts or stops the other as well.

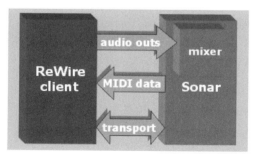

ReWire allows a client's timing, MIDI, and audio functions to integrate seamlessly with a host.

The programs also run in parallel, so if the client program has a sequencer that triggers its sounds, you can add digital audio hard disk and/or MIDI tracks in Sonar. Conversely, songs recorded in Sonar can take advantage of a client's particular attributes (*e.g.,* soft synths in Project5 or Reason, live performance-oriented looping with Ableton's Live) to augment the arrangement. These instrument outputs can go through Sonar's DirectX processors, and of course, you can still use DXi devices within Sonar to expand the soft synth possibilities even further. I've even had good luck inserting more than one ReWire application into Sonar, which *really* surprised me.

ReWire started with Propellerhead Software, but has since become a true industry standard. Not only are more ReWire compatible applications appearing, some pre-ReWire applications have been updated for ReWire compatibility.

Computer Requirements

ReWire itself doesn't use up much CPU power; it is simply an interconnection protocol. However, as you'll be using two programs together, your computer needs enough power to run them both comfortably. Generally, this means a decent amount of RAM (*e.g.,* 512 MB) and a fast processor (1 GHz is a good start, although a slower one can work if you don't make too many demands on it).

Software synthesizers tend to require a lot of CPU power, as do signal processors. However, there are ways to reduce the amount of CPU power needed, as described in the chapter on Plug-Ins.

Recommended Drivers

Although ReWire will sorta work with Sonar using MME drivers, WDM or ASIO drivers provide greatly increased efficiency and far lower latency (*i.e.,* the delay between the time you trigger a note, and when you actually hear it). Check your sound card manufacturer's web site to see if WDM or ASIO drivers are available for your card. Using Sonar without low-latency drivers is like driving a Porsche without ever getting out of second gear—you can do it, but why would you want to?

Note that you do not need to install any additional hardware or software to use ReWire, as it is an entirely software-based function that is built within ReWire-compatible programs. There may be a few rules you need to follow, like closing or opening programs in a particular order, but no custom drivers or other software accessories are needed.

Sharing MIDI I/O

The documentation implies Sonar can't share MIDI I/O with other programs, but that's true only if you're using simple MIDI I/O and want to drive each program independently. For example, I use Reason and Sonar together and have no trouble driving Sonar when it has the focus, and Reason when it has the focus, as it gets its MIDI data from Sonar (in a sense, Sonar provides the "MIDI Thru" to Reason). The bottom line is you can play notes in Reason using the same MIDI port and connections that you use to record notes in Sonar.

ReWire Setup

Let's look at how to use Sonar with a few different ReWire programs. For this tutorial, we'll assume your setup has:

- A single MIDI controller
- A MIDI interface with a single input port

This is the least flexible setup for running any client as a stand-alone program, as it may complicate the issue of remote parameter control for the client. But even this minimal setup works fine for integrating a ReWire program with Sonar.

SETTING UP THE REWIRE CLIENT

I've tested Sonar and ReWire using Cakewalk Project5, Propellerhead Reason, Arturia Storm, and Ableton Live. Regardless of whatever assignments are under audio and MIDI preferences in these programs, as soon as you insert one of them into Sonar as a ReWire client, ReWire takes over and sets the audio, sync, and MIDI parameters automatically. Sweet!

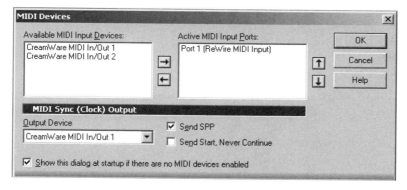

As with other well-written ReWire clients, Project5 automatically optimizes its MIDI setup for ReWire applications as soon as you insert it into Sonar.

Setting Up Sonar

1. Go *Options* > *MIDI Devices.*
2. Verify that Sonar's desired MIDI in and out ports are highlighted, and located at the top of the "MIDI Devices" list. If a desired port is not at the top of the list, click on the port to highlight it, then click on "Move Selected Devices to Top."

The MIDI ports you want to use should be highlighted and moved to the top.

3. Go *Options* > *Audio* > "Advanced" tab. Under "Playback and Recording," uncheck "Share Drivers with Other Programs."

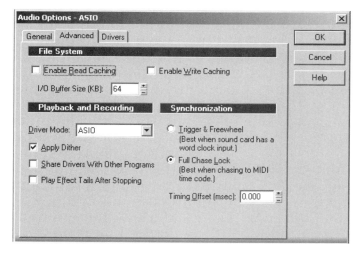

Sharing drivers is not a good idea, because switching to other programs could mute Sonar's outputs. Although you can get out of this by shifting the focus back to Sonar or initiating playback on the ReWire slave or master, it's easier to make the change in Preferences and not have to think about it any more.

Inserting a ReWire Device Into Sonar

The most important rules to remember are:

- When starting a project, open Sonar first. Do not have the client program open when you open Sonar. Insert the client only after Sonar is open.

- When finishing a project, close the client program first, then close Sonar. Doing the reverse won't cause any damage, but you'll be told to close the client first.

To insert the ReWire device:

1. Go *Insert > ReWire Device > [ReWire device name]*.
2. The Insert Synth Options dialog appears. Here's what each box means.

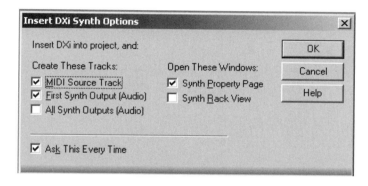

Use this window to specify how Sonar will handle clients with multiple outputs.

- **MIDI Source Track**—Check this, as it creates a MIDI track for driving the ReWire application.
- **First Synth Output (Audio)**—If you check this, Sonar adds two audio tracks that carry the client program's mixed stereo output. This is recommended for when you first get into using ReWire.
- **All Synth Outputs (Audio)**—Checking this causes Sonar to create a separate audio track for each of the available audio outputs in a client. For example, in the case of Reason, this means the 64 outs in the "hardware interface" (at the top of the Reason rack). This is recommended for advanced users, as we'll explain later.
- **Synth Property Page**—The client interface opens up automatically. I'd recommend checking this for convenience.
- **Synth Rack View**—This calls up the Synth Rack window. I generally leave this unchecked to avoid "window clutter"; you can always go *View > Synth Rack* if you want to see it.

- **Ask This Every Time**—I usually leave this checked because sometimes I want First Synth Output, and sometimes I want All Synth Outputs, depending on the project.

After making your selections, click on "OK." It takes a few moments to load up and insert a ReWire client, so be patient if it seems nothing is happening for a few seconds.

PROGRAM-SPECIFIC COMMENTS

ReWire is quite stable, but it's a young protocol and you may encounter a few issues when you first try it. Here are some hints for specific programs, but remember, fixes may occur in future revisions and these cautions may no longer apply.

Reason

If upon inserting Reason within Sonar you see an error message that says "MIDI Input Problem," simply ignore it. The programs know what to do.

Sonar handles all MIDI control for Reason. To play a Reason instrument via MIDI, go to Sonar's "MIDI Ch" parameter, and select the desired instrument from the drop-down menu.

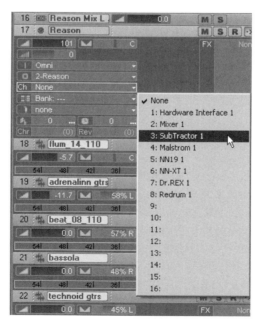

Select the instrument you want to play; Sonar will "thru" any MIDI controller info to the selected Reason instrument.

Live

When you insert Live, Sonar creates the corresponding audio and MIDI tracks and recognizes that Live is running as a ReWire client. However, at least in my setup, the Live program screen does not appear. The fix is simply to open Live *after* it has been inserted.

APPLICATIONS

Let's verify that your computer is up to the task and all is working well. From there, we can move on to more advanced applications.

Testing ReWire

1. If you haven't already set up Sonar as described above, do so now.
2. Close both the ReWire client and Sonar if either one is open.
3. Open Sonar. For now, just close out of the Sonar Quick Start dialog to retain the default project (2 audio and 2 MIDI tracks).
4. Go *Insert > ReWire Device,* and select the ReWire client application.
5. The "Insert DXi Synth Options" window appears. Refer to the section "Inserting a ReWire Device Into Sonar" for general guidance on which boxes to check or uncheck. For now, check "MIDI Source Track," "First Synth Output," "Synth Property Page," and "Ask This Every Time." Leave "All Synth Outputs" and "Synth Rack View" unchecked.
6. After selecting your options, click on "OK."
7. The client will open with either a default configuration or the last configuration used.
8. Give Sonar the focus. While inserting the client, Sonar creates a stereo audio track for the client's mixer outs and a MIDI track to drive any instruments (or provide MIDI control functions) that are placed below any existing Sonar tracks. For example, with the Normal Sonar template, these show up as tracks 5 and 6 respectively.
9. Test the setup by clicking on Sonar's "Play" button. If the client loaded a default song, it will play back in tandem with Sonar. Otherwise, change the focus between Sonar and the client; both transports should be doing their thing. Whether you'll hear anything varies from program to program; for example, with Live, you have to enable a Live Clip for triggering before it can play back under Sonar (just as if you were using Live by itself).
10. Change Sonar's tempo. The client's tempo will change to the tempo you selected.
11. Check the VU meters; they should indicate any audio that the client is producing.

If you didn't encounter any problems in the above steps, ReWire is working with the selected client.

Sonar's Multi-Timbral Synth Rack

A ReWire client like Reason, Project5, Storm, etc. makes a great synth rack for Sonar. ReWire the program into Sonar, and create individual MIDI tracks for each instrument you want to make part of your Sonar arrangement.

With Project5, there are a few ways to get synths to play back from Sonar tracks, but here's what works best for me.

1. In Sonar, select "Project5" as the "Output" parameter for each MIDI channel you want to use.
2. Again in Sonar, choose a MIDI channel for each track with the "Ch" parameter.
3. In Project5, in the info strip above a selected instrument, select "No Ports" for Input MIDI Port, and match the MIDI channel to the MIDI channel assignment for the corresponding track in Sonar.
4. Remember to Ctrl-click on the MIDI jacks to the left of an instrument name in P5's "tracks pane" to enable its MIDI input.

With Reason, select "Reason" as the MIDI track's output, then select the desired Reason instrument with the "Ch" parameter. As you keep adding tracks of Reason instruments, note that you can trigger notes for any of the instruments by just clicking on the appropriate Sonar track. This makes it very easy to do overdubs, or tweak Reason's parameters.

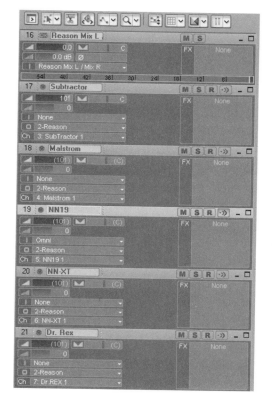

Five MIDI tracks have been created in Sonar, each one driving a particular Reason device. Initiating recording on one of these tracks will record the MIDI data needed to drive the respective virtual instruments.

Also note that the ReWire implementation has a special feature: If you record a track that's assigned to ReDrum, Sonar's Piano Roll inserts the drum names for notes—you don't need to create a drum map to see which notes correspond to which drum sounds.

In Reason, I've created a default synth rack for Sonar, named it "Basic ReWire Rack.rns," stored it in Reason's "Template Songs" folder, and made it Reason's default file (why use Reason's sequencer when Sonar's is so much easier?). Here's how to set a specific file as a default in Reason.

1. In Reason, go *Edit > Preferences*.
2. Under Default Song, click the "Custom" radio button.
3. Click on the "Folder" icon (on the same line as the "Custom" button).
4. Navigate to the "Template Songs" folder and click on the "Basic ReWire Rack.rns" file you created, then click on "Open."
5. Close Preferences.

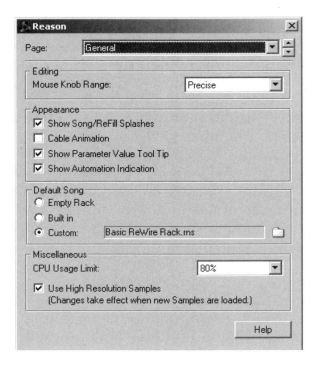

You can create a basic synth rack in Reason, and make it the default file so that it loads whenever you ReWire Reason into Sonar.

Recording Reason Controller Tweaks in Real Time

How controllers are automated depends on your setup. The Sonar documentation says that Reason and Sonar cannot share MIDI I/O, however this is not necessarily true. Sharing I/O does place some limitations with respect to using Reason's MIDI Remote control option to adjust parameters, but there are workarounds for this. The following applies to a setup using one MIDI controller, one MIDI port, and some assignable controller knobs (*e.g.,* mod wheel, data slider, etc. that can be assigned to different controller numbers).

With this type of setup, you can do real-time tweaking of any parameter listed in Reason's MIDI implementation chart (this is an Adobe Acrobat-compatible PDF file included on the Reason CD; if you did the standard installation, it's accessible from *Start > Programs > Propellerheads > Reason > MIDI Implementation Charts*).

Please note that the process we're about to describe does not involve using Reason's "MIDI Remote" option, which is how we get away with using a single MIDI port.

For example, suppose you want to automate SubTractor's "Amplitude Envelope Decay" parameter. Here's how.

1. Refer to the MIDI Implementation chart and find the Amp Env Decay parameter. This is controlled via MIDI Controller #9.
2. Assign the controller you plan to use so that it transmits data over Controller #9.
3. Switch over to Reason, then move the control knob or slider you want to use. SubTractor's Amp Env Decay slide should follow your motions.
4. Record the track normally in Sonar while playing notes and/or tweaking the control knob. After you stop, you'll see the note and controller data in the Clips Pane.
5. Switch over to Reason and rewind back to the beginning, then press "Play" (or do this in Sonar, then switch over to Reason). The part will play back, and you'll see Reason's Amp Env Decay follow the controller data.

Some parameters you might want to automate (specifically, "Filter Frequency," "Filter Resonance," "LFO 1 Amount," "Phase Difference," and "FM Amount") can be tied in with the mod wheel; each also has an "Amount" parameter that determines how much the mod wheel affects the parameter.

If you want to modulate only one of these parameters, no problem. Use the listed MIDI controller number, or set the parameter's corresponding Amount knob (in the bend/mod wheel section) for the desired maximum amount of modulation when the mod wheel is up full, then record mod wheel motion into the MIDI track. For example, to modulate the Filter Frequency with the mod wheel, turn up the "F. Freq" control as desired, then record the wheel motions.

Furthermore, independent modulation for these parameters is also possible because each of the "Amount" knobs in the bend/mod wheel section can be MIDI-controlled. Therefore, if you set the mod wheel amount to maximum, you can then modulate the "Amount" controls to tweak specific parameters individually. For example, modulating the "F. Freq" control (which responds to MIDI Controller #33) will vary the filter cutoff, while modulating the "LFO1 Mod Wheel Amount "(MIDI Controller #35) will modulate that parameter independently.

Using Multiple Outputs with ReWire

This is an advanced application that lets clients with multiple outputs have each instrument output show up as a separate Sonar track, rather than feeding them all into a stereo mix. Therefore, each instrument can have it own audio processing, and track data (level, pan, effects send, etc.) automation within Sonar.

Be aware, though, that selecting all outputs can be a lot of outputs. With Reason, there are 64 outputs; with Project5, there are outputs for the main audio, four auxes, and 59 possible synth outputs to accommodate those synths with multiple outputs.

Here's how to set up Sonar and the client for multiple outputs.

1. When you insert the ReWire client, uncheck "First Synth Output (Audio)" and check "All Synth Outputs (Audio)."
2. Sonar inserts the client, then creates as many audio tracks as there are client outputs. Be patient—this might take a while.
3. With Project5, as you insert synths, their outputs will correspond to tracks in Sonar. A number to the right of the synth name (in P5's "tracks pane") relates to the Sonar track number. Note that as you select a different set of outputs with multiple-output instruments in P5, this number changes to show which track is being fed. With Reason, use its patch bay to connect the instruments in your Reason rack to the desired outputs.
4. To unclutter the Tracks Pane, hide tracks that correspond to unused outputs (while in the Track or Console View, access the Track Manager to show/hide tracks with the "M" keyboard shortcut).

Project5 has been rewired into Sonar using multiple outputs. Note the numbers to the right of the instrument names in Project5; they correspond to the track numbers in Sonar.

Playing REX Files in Sonar

Sonar's on the fly time-stretching abilities let you use loops of various tempos and have them all work together—very cool.

Another method of accomplishing a similar result was devised by Propellerhead Software several years ago, called the REX file format. As mentioned in the chapter "Loops and Loop Recording," this file format "slices" a piece of digital audio into several pieces, and triggers them based on their position in a sequence. Thus, if the sequence slows down, the triggers occur further apart and the slices play back at a slower rate. The reverse occurs if the sequencer speeds up.

Quite a few sequencers that lack built-in time-stretching can read REX files, and as a result, there are numerous sample CDs with REX format loops. Although Sonar currently doesn't read REX files, until it does there's a simple workaround if you run Reason as a ReWire device.

There are two main options:

- Create a sequence in Reason that triggers REX files stored in Reason's Dr. Rex file playback module (remember, under ReWire, the Sonar and Reason transports are locked together).
- Create a sequence in Sonar that drives the REX file.

For situations where you're using Reason's stereo mixed outputs instead of one-track-per-instrument, the second option is far more flexible because if the Reason Dr. Rex files loop continuously, then you'll need to use track automation to change the Dr. Rex levels. Yet any changes made to the stereo outs will affect any other instruments feeding those outs. When Dr. Rex is driven by a MIDI file in Sonar, you can modify the data within Sonar—for example, just cut out a chunk if you want the sound to go away, or edit velocities to change dynamics. Here's one way to do REX files in Sonar.

1. Set up Sonar and Reason to function as ReWire devices.
2. Have at least one Dr. Rex module in your Reason rack.
3. Use Dr. Rex's Browse option (accessed by clicking on the folder icon) to find a REX file you want to use. If you don't hear any sound, make sure Sonar's Audio Engine is on (the engine button in the transport bar should be "pushed in"; if not, click on it).
4. After finding a sound you want to use, load it into the Dr. Rex module that currently has the focus.

5. Some sample CDs with REX files also include a companion MIDI file for triggering the audio slices at the right times. If not, you can create one. In Reason, go *File > Export Rex as MIDI File,* and click on "Save."

Now Reason is set up. Let's proceed to Sonar.

1. Locate the MIDI file you just created, or the corresponding one from the sample CD, and drag it into a Sonar MIDI track. Or, use Sonar's "Open" command to bring the MIDI file into a new document, then drag the file over from there.
2. Make the correct assignments for Reason on the Sonar MIDI track. The "Out" parameter should say "Reason," and Channel should show the name of the currently selected Dr. Rex module in Reason.
3. Copy and paste the MIDI data as desired to play back the REX file.

Press "Play" in Sonar (or Reason, whatever works for you), and the MIDI data in the Sonar track will play back the "slices" of digital audio in Reason's Dr. Rex file player.

9

BACKUP AND DOCUMENTATION

Do you back up everything? Sure, of course you do.

Well actually, many people don't learn the lesson of proper backup until they lose more work than they can ever hope to re-create. The resulting loss of time and money from a critical hard disk failure can be devastating to a small studio or business.

There's an old saying that "digital data isn't real unless it exists in more than one place." But backing up is not quite that simple. To understand why, consider that the purpose of backing up is not only to prevent you from experiencing a loss of data you use in the present, but also to allow you to use that data in the future. And that's where things get interesting: You need to back up to the most universal format possible, and do extensive documentation.

THE UNIVERSAL BACKUP

Let's assume you're conscientious about backing up, and when you finish a project, you immediately save everything as a bundle file, or you back up the per-project folder to a medium like CD-R, DVD+R or DVD-R, tape drive, or removable hard drive. Your job is done, right?

Not necessarily. When you need to open your files five or ten years from now because someone wants to do a remix or reissue, the media may be fine, Sonar may recognize the file, and all seems ready to go...until you find that several plug-ins won't load, because they're not compatible with Windows a few generations down the line, or you switched to a different computer and authorization was tied to your original hard drive (worse yet, the company may have gone out of business, precluding re-authorization).

Weird problems can happen too. I tried to pull up a project in Sonar 2.2, but it said it couldn't load plug-ins that I knew were installed on my system— older files, using the same plug-ins, loaded without a hitch. Was there file corruption? Did I rename the plug-ins and not remember that I did? I'll never know. But this made me realize that simply backing up is not good enough.

The most universal backup format is to save each track as an individual WAV file—I think that even a decade from now, programs will be able to at the very least import WAV files. This also yields the greatest possible compatibility with other programs.

The drag-and-save technique seems ideal for this concept: Select all tracks, drag them to a folder, back up the folder to multiple media, and *voilà*— you're protected. But there's more you need to do.

First, all the tracks must have a common starting point, so you can time-align them when you import them into your DAW. Therefore, any track you save should extend from the song's beginning to the end of whatever's recorded on the track. You can do this by selecting all the Clips in a track and going Edit > Bounce to Clip(s). This fuses them all into a single Clip whose length extends from the left-most Clip to the right-most (if there are gaps between Clips, they are rendered as silence). Grab the left-most edge of the composite Clip, and drag it out to the beginning of the song. Then (important!), select the Clip and go *Edit > Bounce to Clip(s)* a second time so that this extra space becomes part of the Clip as well.

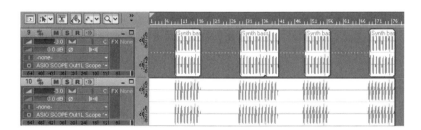

The upper track consists of a number of Clips. The lower track is a clone of the upper track, but with all Clips selected, then bounced to a single Clip. The beginning has also been extended to the start of the song. Gaps between Clips appear in the bounced Clip as silence.

If you don't bounce all a track's Clips to a single Clip, there are additional issues. If you select each Clip and drag-and-save, each will be saved as a separate file, with no obvious temporal relationship (Broadcast WAV file time-stamping should take care of this, but let's assume a worse-case scenario.)

• Backup and Documentation •

Furthermore, when you drag a slip-edited Clip over, the *entire* Clip gets saved—even any hidden parts. In some ways this is good, because you can go back and "open up" the Clip to reveal the edited part. But it doesn't help in terms of backing up individual tracks, only the Clips that comprise them.

Also, automation moves, automation envelopes, Clip envelopes, and the effects of any signal processing are not saved with a drag-and-save operation—only the raw Clip data. While this is ideal for remixers, you may want the file to include some of these elements, which brings us to...

Exporting Tracks as Audio

The best solution for a truly universal backup is to export each hard disk track individually (we'll deal with MIDI tracks and virtual instruments in a bit). To do this, select only the track to export (I also solo it for added security), and select the range to be exported (*i.e.*, from the beginning of the song to the end of the track). The signal comes from the Source Bus being fed by the track, so to be absolutely safe, play the track all the way through to make sure that both the track and bus meters don't indicate excessively high or low level.

If the levels are fine, double-check that you've selected the correct range, then go *File > Export > Audio*. You'll see a dialog box that determines the exported track's characteristics.

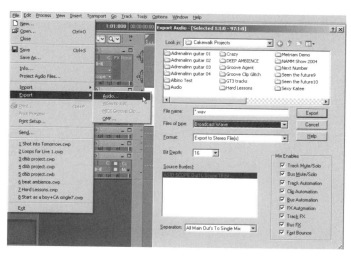

The "Export Audio" dialog box lets you choose the file format and type, along with bit depth and "mix enables." These come in handy when you want to save multiple versions of the same track— one with automation, one without, one with processing, one with no plug-ins, etc.

Note the "Mix Enables" options. These are important because you may want to save multiple versions of a track. For example, perhaps the reverb plug-in you used on the original vocal track will sound pretty bad compared to what a native reverb will be able to do in 2012. In that case, you'll be glad you saved a version without reverb. Ditto automation: It's prudent to save a version of a file with automation moves and one without, in case you change your mind about the mix and need to make some changes.

Virtual Instruments

Render any virtual instrument outputs to an audio track, which can also be saved as a file. We covered how to do this earlier in the chapter on plug-ins, but the basic idea is to drag across the range you want to mix down, in the time line above the tracks. Then solo both the track containing the soft synth audio and the related MIDI track driving the soft synth. In the Tracks Pane, Ctrl-click on both track numbers so that they're both selected, play the part and check the track and bus meters for overload, then export as described above.

MIDI

We're not done yet: Part of the backup should include any MIDI data that drives virtual instruments or provides controller data. Just use the *File > Save As* function to save the song, choose the MIDI file format (I recommend MIDI Format 1 as it saves each channel to its own track), then click on "Save." When it's time to resurrect a file from the past, you may be able to replace the wheezy soft synth you always hated with something new and wonderful—but only if you saved the MIDI part that tells the synth what to do.

Before assuming all is well, open up the resulting file and make sure that the tracks are labelled in such a way that it's obvious which track drives which soft synth. In fact, you really should document the entire tune in as much detail as humanly possible, which we'll cover soon.

Sonar's Bundle Format

And while you're at it, save the song using Sonar's Bundle file format (.CWB suffix). Although this format is readable only by Sonar, it contains all audio and project data needed to re-create the file, assuming you have the appropriate plug-ins. This makes it useful not only for your own use, but for exchanging with other Sonar users.

Space Issues

Saving out all these files translates into a fair amount of material. Let's say you've done a 4-minute pop tune with 32 tracks, using 16-bit resolution at 44.1 kHz. Each track will take about 40 MB (or 60 MB for 24-bit files). 32 tracks equals 1,280 MB, and if you save alternate versions of the tracks (e.g., with or without automation), you can double or triple that. Where are you going to save all this stuff?

You currently have five main options:

- **DVD+R or DVD-R.** These formats hold a little under 5 GB, so you can hold all your material on a single disc (I advise one song per disc any-way—that way if there's a catastrophic physical problem with the media, you've lost only one song).

- **CD-R.** At 700 MB, you may need several of these to back up your materi-al. But they're cheap, proven, and it's likely you can find something that can read them back a few years from now.

- **Data tape.** I'm not that big a fan of tape backup. It's cost-effective and fairly reliable, but I have concerns about finding devices that can play back those tapes a decade from now.

- **Big hard drive.** Put a removable drive bay in your computer, buy a 120 GB drive, and make it a removable backup drive. A drive like this can cost a little over $100, and stores a lot of tunes.

- **Red Book Audio CD.** Should all else fail, if you back up each track as its own song, you can always play the audio output into something.

But don't back up to only one medium. For example, back up to both DVD+R and hard disk, with Red Book Audio just to be safe. Keep the hard drive or DVD+R in a safe deposit box, and every few years, "refresh" them to new media (I just saved all my DAT tapes to CD-R).

Yes, it's a lot to store (but think about 2" reels of analog tape, and you won't feel so bad!). Is it really worth saving all this data? Only you can decide. But I've been in this business long enough to see a lot of music get resurrected, so when in doubt, it pays to save.

THE JOY OF SYSEX

With some projects, I like to send Sonar's outs through a dual light-pipe ADAT interface, and mix on a digital mixer (mostly so I can have lots of faders and controls, but also to be able to use analog effects with the mixer's aux buses). As a result, the mixer settings become part of the tune, and need to be restored for any subsequent editing or remixing—and if they need to be restored, then they need to be backed up somewhere. The same is true of using any external gear: There should be some way to back up their settings *within* the Sonar project, should there be a need to restore the settings later on.

Luckily, there's an easy way to do this for any gear that supports MIDI sysex (system exclusive) data. Sonar has a sophisticated sys ex capture/editing/playback options, but let's keep it simple and just cover how to save sys ex with a Sonar project, and have it reload the sys ex into target instruments when you start that project.

1. Patch a MIDI cable between the source MIDI device output and the Sonar MIDI input (as selected in *Options* > *MIDI Devices*).
2. Go *Options* > *Global* > *MIDI* and make sure "System Exclusive" is checked.
3. Go *View* > *Sysx*. This shows 8,192 banks of sys ex. A bank could be something like a complete synth setup, a particular program, mixer preset, etc.
4. Click on the red arrow (receive sys ex) or type "C." At this point, you'll see a menu with a plethora of supported synths. If your device happens to be on this list, select it and click on "OK." From this point on, the process is pretty much automatic.
5. If a device is not on the list, select "You start dump on instrument" and click on "OK."
6. A screen appears that shows sys ex reception status. It should read "0 bytes received," followed by the available space for sys ex storage.
7. Initiate the dump on the source instrument. You may need to dig in the instrument's manual to find which button will initiate the bulk data dump.
8. The counter will increment as Sonar receives the data. When the counter stops, the sys ex has been received; click on "Done."
9. The toolbar at the top of the Sysx view window is now fully functional. Click on the "abc" button to name the bank (always a good idea!)

• Backup and Documentation •

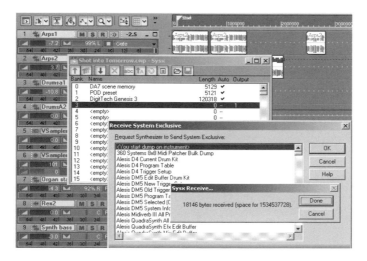

Here are the three main screens involved in receiving sys ex. The front window shows the amount of sys ex data that's been received. The window just behind it is where you initiate the actual request to accept sys ex data; the rear-most window shows the sys ex banks, and the toolbar for managing this data.

If you now save the Project, the sys ex data will be part of it. You can do three things with the stored sys ex bank:

- Save it to disk as a sys ex file (click on the floppy disk icon, navigate where to want to save, then save).
- Send the bank to a target device (click on the black arrow at the left)
- Send the bank automatically when you open the project

Here's how to do automatic bank sends:

1. In the Sysx view, highlight the bank you want to send automatically.
2. Click on the "Auto Send Bank" button (black arrow and letter A). This places a check mark in the "Auto" column for the selected bank.
3. Save the Project file so it contains this additional information.
4. The next time you open the project, a screen will appear while loading and remind you that the file contains sys ex data that is supposed to be sent automatically to your MIDI gear. To send it, click "OK," otherwise click on "Cancel."

You can disable this screen so it doesn't appear by unchecking "Ask this question every time." I leave it checked, though—sometimes you don't want to overwrite works in progress, and it helps to be reminded you're about to blast new data into RAM.

It's extremely convenient to store all the presets for your outboard gear in the same file as your main data. If you haven't taken advantage of this feature, get into the habit of doing so.

DOCUMENTATION

Part of backing up is documenting what you backed up. For example, multiple takes may seem like a good idea at the time, but unless you weed out the unused bits or are very good about a convention for naming, it will be quite a task to sort them out in the future. And if you've saved sys ex for MIDI gear, note the version number of that gear at the time the sys ex was saved—as well as info on the hardware used for recording, notes on performers or mics used, who did the engineering, and so on. Document the session as if someone could walk in cold 15 years from now, load up the folder with your song and documentation, and know exactly how to proceed.

Sonar has a couple useful tools that expedite the process of documenting your session.

The Sonar Notepad

There's no need to document a session in a separate word processor document. Go *File > Info,* and you can enter all kinds of information about the project such as lyrics, recording notes, historical details, etc., as well as view file statistics. You're limited to about 27,000 characters, but that's a lot of info—figure about 4,500 words. Surely that should be enough to document your masterpiece.

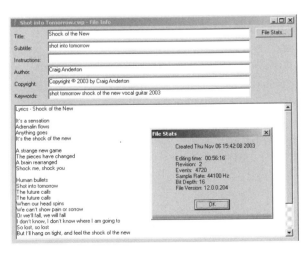

The File Info area is great for taking notes, as well as seeing a project's vital stats.

The Track Notepad

You don't need much for a track name—"Lead 1,""Kick," or whatever. Sometimes, though, it's helpful to include text notes with it, like the patch number used with a synth to create the audio, signal processor presets used with outboard gear (not everyone uses plug-ins), or whatever. While you could always enter this info in Sonar's main notepad, sometimes it's more convenient to be able to look at the pertinent track and see what you need to know.

Sonar lets you enter *very* long track names. Drag the divider between the Clips Pane and Tracks Pane to show as much of the Tracks Pane as possible, then drag the name field divider (located to the left of the Volume slider) toward the right. Drag as far as needed to extend the track name field. Enter the track name and any other info.

The track name field in Sonar can be extended to the point where you can enter performance notes and other information, then hide it to avoid taking up too much of your workspace.

You can even type past the end of the field, and it will scroll to accommodate your typing, up to 138 characters. Make sure to put the most important text first, as that's what will be visible when you reduce the track name field back to something rational.

Dragging to extend the track name field for one track extends it for all tracks, so if you need to sneak a peek at your notes, you can do so for the entire tune. If you can't see the entire text for the line, double-click on it as if you were going to edit it, then drag the cursor left or right to scroll through the additional text.

There's also a cool shortcut. Even if the name field is pulled back so it's very short, place your mouse over the name field, and a pop-up shows most (if not all) of what you've written.

*Merely positioning your mouse over the track name can show a significant amount of "hidden"
text (created by extending the track name field and typing in it).*

MANAGING AND SAVING PLUG-IN DATA

Go *Tools > Sonar Plug-In Manager* to call up a very useful accessory that
made its debut in Sonar's second generation. It lists five "filter" categories,
including DirectShow Audio (DirectX plug-ins), MIDI Effects Filters (MFX),
DirectX Instruments, DirectX Media Objects, and Control Surfaces.

PIM does many things, but one item—hide plug-ins from Sonar—is particularly handy if you have a plug-in installed as both VST and DirectX. If both
versions of the plug-ins show up under Audio Effects, you can hide the VST
or DX version, and save yourself some menu space.

There's also a way to manage presets, although this applies only to newer
plug-ins included with Sonar (including, of course, the Sonitus:fx suite). You
can see a list of presets associated with any Cakewalk plug-in from the five
categories, and rename or delete individual presets.

Those who share work with other Sonarians, or who need to archive all
aspects of a project, will really like the import/export preset feature. Suppose
you have a set of Sonitus:fx Compressor presets you use for vocals. If you're
doing a session somewhere else with Sonar and want to retain your famous
signature vocal sounds, export the presets before you leave your studio to a
floppy, memory stick, etc.; at the other studio, load the presets via the Preset
Manager and they'll be available to the plug-in. You can also save them as
backup for your own work, load different "families" of presets for different
types of projects, and save presets for multiple plug-ins in one file (or even
all presets for all plug-ins to back up all the presets used in a particular project). Note that this works only for user presets, not built-in ones.

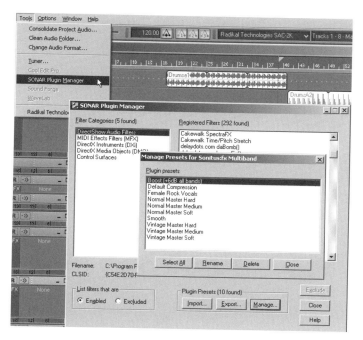

The Plug-In Manager is a very useful tool. Here, the presets for the Sonitus:fx Multiband plug-in are shown; "Boost" is currently selected.

Finally, you can change plug-in names. This works with any plug-in from any company, so if you have three plug-ins called "Chorus," you can make their names more distinctive. Furthermore, other programs reference the new names as well.

AUTOMATIC SAVING

Under *Options > Global >* "General" tab, the third line up from the bottom determines Sonar's auto-save parameters. You can have Sonar save a file automatically after a certain number of minutes have elapsed since the last save, or after a certain number of edit changes. The latter is helpful if you do a flurry of edits (*e.g.*, narration editing) during a very short period of time, and want to make sure you don't lose them.

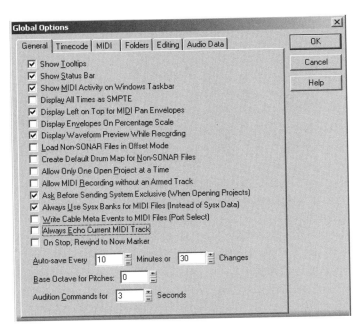

If you're the kind of person who forgets to save periodically, you'll appreciate Sonar's auto-save feature. Just make sure you don't accidentally overwrite an older version you meant to keep.

However, there is a major caution here. Suppose you've saved a file, then decide you want to try some additional edits to see if they work out. If they don't, it doesn't matter because you have the saved version...right? Well, if Sonar auto-saves the new data over the old data, you won't be able to go back to where you were before.

As a result, I strongly suggest saving the file you're working on under a different name periodically. Auto-save will continue to save the most current version, but you'll be able to go back to an older version if desired.

Chapter 10

MASTERING AND SAMPLE/LOOP EDITING

A common question I receive goes something like this: "I've been working with Sonar and everything is recorded just as I want, with perfect reproduction. But on playback, it just does not sound the same as recordings I hear on, radio, CDs etc.—something is missing. I define what I hear from radio or from commercial quality CDs as more 'polished,' a sound that has depth without reverb, presence without volume, solid bass and treble without having to adjust the tone controls."

The issue here is mastering, which is a fairly complex subject. If you want an overview of the process, check out my book "Quick Start Audio Mastering" (in the Music Sales/Wizoo QuickStart series). In most cases you will add a bit of EQ and compression, in that order, to even out the frequency response and dynamic range.

Most mastering is done in a digital audio editing program such as Steinberg Wavelab, Sony Digital Pictures' Sound Forge, Adobe Audition, Magix Sequoia, etc. (and BIAS Peak or TC Electronics' Spark on the Mac). These are optimized for editing applications, including mastering.

But do you really need a separate mastering program if you have Sonar? After all, you can zoom way in on the waveform, cut and rearrange various parts, create a master bus into which all the signals feed, and insert plug-ins into that master bus to process the entire tune. Sonar Producer also includes two plug-ins suitable for mastering: Sonitus fx:Multiband for dynamics processing, and Sonitus fx:Equalizer for tone control.

The answer depends on your needs. If you intend to do a CD-quality release, I would definitely recommend a separate mastering program. A multitracked song with plug-ins will use up a lot of processing power, and high-quality mastering processors that also require a reasonable amount of CPU power might put things over the edge (you want to use plug-ins for mastering whose prime directive is highest possible quality, not miserly CPU consumption).

Also, a "real" mastering program will have better navigation and easier range selection—essential if you're mastering something like narration, and need to do phrase-by-phrase normalization.

However, it's almost a given that mastering will involve some EQ and multi-band compression or loudness maximization. If you've had mastering done professionally, you've probably noticed that these processors change the mix, however subtly. As a result, when mixing tracks, it can be a good idea to insert EQ and a loudness maximizer or multiband compressor in the master bus FX slot, with moderate settings. This way, the mix reflects some of the changes that will likely occur during mastering.

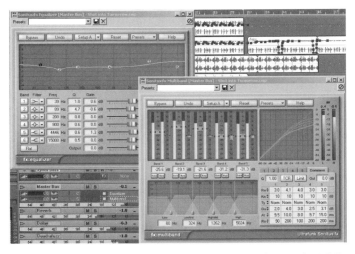

The Sonitus: fx Equalizer and Multiband are inserted in the master bus FX slot. While setting up a mix, this allows the mix to reflect some of the changes that are likely to occur during mastering. Use very light amounts of EQ and compression to start, as they have more apparent effect on program material than on individual tracks.

I then render the mix to stereo WAV, but *without* the mastering plug-ins. For the "real" mastering, I bring the WAV file into a digital audio editing program and work there. However, since using mastering processors as part of the mixing process, I haven't found it necessary to go back and change the mix in order to compensate for changes that happen while mastering.

WAVEFORM EDITING

Sonar is a wonderful tool for developing and even mastering sample libraries. I record "backing tracks" in Sonar so that when creating samples, I can actually play along with something; I think this gives a better "feel," and keeps the sample locked to the rhythm. Also, I generally save to the Acidized WAV format, which Sonar has supported since V2.0.

When recording loops designed for relatively high BPMs, although I practice at the higher tempo, the final version gets recorded around 90-100 BPM so that it can time-stretch over the widest possible range (Acidized files sound better sped up than slowed down). As the backing tracks are also Acidized (or MIDI files), shifting tempo during the sample creation process is not a problem.

What *is* a problem is bouncing the samples back and forth between Sonar and a digital audio editor for more detailed editing, as the constant shuffling can get tedious. Can the required sample editing could be done within Sonar? While there are definitely limitations compared to a dedicated digital audio editor (no pencil-type tool for waveform drawing, less detailed calibrations, no built-in analysis options, etc.), Sonar handily covers the basics. In fact, for some applications it compensates for any deficiencies by streamlining the process required to go from recording though editing, mastering, and ultimately, using it in a track.

Setting Up the Right View

Sample editing is easier with a large waveform view, so set the Track Pane's horizontal divider so only the main output bus is visible at the bottom; the area above that serves as the waveform display. If you're working mostly with one track and want to quickly maximize the waveform view, select the track, then type "H" (or go to "View Options" and select "Show Only Selected Tracks"). I also hide the Inspector to gain more screen real estate (toggle the Inspector show/hide by typing "I"). To go back to showing all tracks, type "A."

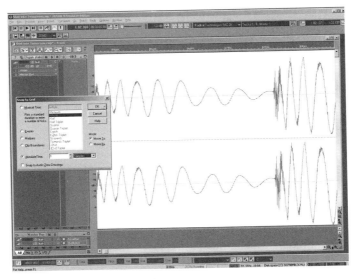

For waveform editing, expand the waveform to as large a view as possible. Note the Time Ruler here is calibrated in samples; the number to the left of the "Audio Running" indicator at the bottom shows the value, in samples, of the cursor's current location. Snap to grid has been set for the highest possible resolution: snap to individual samples, with "Snap to Audio Zero Crossings" turned off.

If you want to be able to do waveform editing on lots of tracks in a project, here's how to toggle between minimum track height and the maximum possible for viewing purposes.

1. Select all tracks (with the focus on the Tracks Pane, go *Edit > Select > All*, or type "Ctrl-A").
2. While holding the "Shift" key, drag the top track's lower edge so it takes up the entire available waveform view.
3. Release the "Shift" key.
4. Click each track's "Minimize" button.

Now you can set any track to maximum height by clicking on its "Maximize" button, and when you're done editing, return to normal size with "Minimize."

Learn the Keyboard Equivalents

Zooming around a waveform is easier if you know the shortcuts.

Zoom out horizontally = Ctrl + Right Arrow
Zoom in horizontally = Ctrl + Left Arrow
Zoom out vertically = Ctrl + Alt + Down Arrow
Zoom in vertically = Ctrl + Alt + Up Arrow
Zoom to marquee = Hold Z key and drag cursor across desired region

• Mastering and Sample/Loop Editing •

Undo view change = U
Redo view change = Shift + U

As the "U" and "Shift + U" commands have histories, it's easy to go forward or backward through changes in zoom levels, track heights, etc. For example, you could use the zoom-to-marquee function to zoom in tight on a suspected click, then zoom back out to look for the next area that might need help.

Defining Regions

There are four main ways to define a region.

Click and drag in the time ruler. This is quick, but you can't see the area being selected as you select it—you see the region boundaries only after clicking and dragging, then releasing the mouse.

Shift-click a new region boundary. You can easily modify a region by Shift-clicking precisely where you want a region boundary (this can even be sample-accurate if you monitor the cursor position in the sample readout to the left of the Audio Running label on the program's bottom strip). The region extends or shrinks, as appropriate, to place the boundary at the clicked point.

Alt-drag over the Clip waveform. This is the most like a conventional waveform editor, as the region is highlighted while you drag. If you Alt-drag in the time ruler, though, highlighting doesn't occur until you release the mouse.

Using markers. Click on the region start or end (zoom way in for maximum accuracy), then click the "Insert Marker" button (the orange triangle with the +) in the Markers toolbar. You needn't bother naming it, just hit "OK" unless you have a compelling need to identify things.

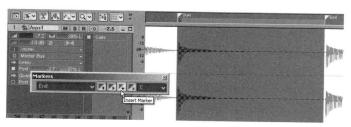

The note at the beginning of beat 2 has been selected as a region for possible normalization by dropping in two markers, labeled "Start" and "End," then clicking between the marker "flags." Note also the "Insert Marker" button, to which the cursor points.

Similarly, drop a marker at the opposite region boundary. Now, you can select the area between the two markers as a region simply by clicking between the two markers in the strip just above the Time Ruler.

The best part is that you can set up multiple markers at several loop points. I usually create loops by playing the part that makes up the loop over and over for several minutes, in a linear fashion. After recording is complete, I solo the track and isolate a few measures at a time to see which potential loop sounds best. By marking off the "candidate" loops, it's easy to compare them: click the region between the markers to select a loop, click on the "Set Loop to Selection" button, then hit "Play."

PRECISION TIMING

If you're creating loops with Sonar, it's best to cut loops to a particular number of samples that relates to the loop tempo (*e.g.*, with a project that runs at 44,100 samples per second, a one-measure loop at 120 BPM lasts two seconds, or 88,200 samples). But even with other types of audio, precision can be crucial (*e.g.*, sound effects for commercials or videos). Sonar allows trimming down to individual samples.

For the most precise timing, call up the Snap to Grid function and select "Absolute Time: 1 Sample." Also select "Move To," and make sure you uncheck "Snap to Audio Zero Crossings." Otherwise, this could mess up a loop's timing because Sonar will snap not necessarily where you want, but to a nearby zero crossing.

Before getting too much into trimming, note that processing a track can cause a slight delay at the track start. I've tested various plug-ins and their inherent delay varies quite a bit, from no delay to a couple dozen samples. So after processing is complete, I head back to the track start, look for a flat line from the beginning to where the signal starts, cut that section out, then slide the loop over so it begins at zero time.

After you've isolated the desired region, trim it. Assuming you want it to be a specific number of measures in length, turn on "Snap to Grid," set it for "Musical Time: Whole," see that "Move To" is still checked, and make sure that "Snap to Audio Zero Crossings" remains *unchecked*. But remember that Sonar usually edits non-destructively, so if you plan the drag the Clip into another folder (or wherever) to save it, you first have to decide how you're going to trim the Clip. There are two ways:

- Slip-edit the Clip by dragging the start and end toward the region's left and right boundaries, respectively. Note that this Clip should not be enabled for looping. Go *Edit > Apply Trimming* to discard anything past the selected region. Saving the Clip saves only the remaining region. This works best for non-looped pieces of digital audio.

- The second method also requires slip-editing to the desired length. But this time, double-click inside the Clip, and the loop construction window opens. Specify the number of beats in the Clip, and Sonar will ask if you want to discard hidden audio beyond the slip edit points; say "Yes." This process is preferable if the region's eventual destiny is to become a loop.

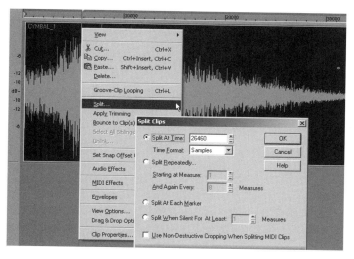

If you have a non-rhythmic sample (e.g., a sound effect) and want to cut it to a specific number of samples, seconds, or measures:beat:ticks, right-click on the Clip and select "Split." In the "Split Clips" dialog box, choose the time format for the split point, and where you want the split to occur. For example, if you want to split at 26,460 samples (exactly 1 beat at 100 BPM), enter "Samples" for "Time Format," and enter "26,460" under "Split at Time."

Chapter 11

1 1

EXPORTING FILES

SUCCESSFUL RENDERING TO WAV

Here's something I've seen on bulletin boards: Someone complains that when they're playing back a tune, everything sounds great. But when they then "render" the tracks to a WAV file on hard disk with the *Edit > Export Audio* function and play back the mixed track, the sound is too soft (or in some cases, so loud that it distorts).

There are many reason why this could be happening, but here's a likely scenario that also reviews the basics of successful exporting in Sonar.

When you export audio (go *File > Export > Audio;* you'll likely want to choose Broadcast WAV as the "Files of Type" format), the signal comes from the bus or buses specified in the "Source Bus(es)" field in the "Export Audio" dialog box. Unless the tracks were cut or mixed at fairly low levels, adding them together will likely overload the output bus. During the mix process, periodically check the output bus meter and make sure that clipping hasn't occurred (as indicated by a lit clip indicator to the right of the bus meter).

Ideally, you want the bus output level to be as hot as possible, short of clipping. Although you can just adjust the level on a trial-and-error basis until it seems right, there's a much more reliable method. This involves setting the bus meters to their highest resolution, and using the peak hold/lock feature.

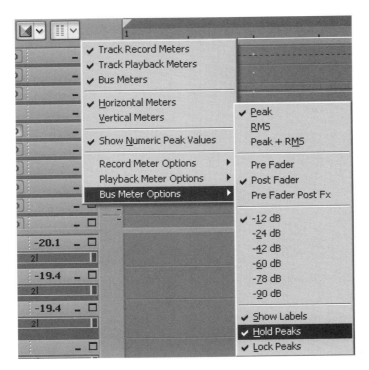

To send the hottest signal level short of distortion to the output bus, choose your bus meter options carefully so you can monitor the output signal as accurately as possible.

1. Click on the "Meter Options" arrow (to the right of the "Show/Hide All Meters" button).
2. Go *Bus Meter Options,* and make sure the following are checked:

- Peak
- Post Fader
- -12 dB
- Show Labels
- Hold Peaks
- Lock Peaks

3. Play the song through, then note the peak values. For example, suppose the peak level for the bus registers -2, as indicated by the number to the left of the Minimize/Maximize buttons (Track Pane), or just below the bus meters (Console View).

4. You now know you are not taking advantage of at least 2 dB of headroom. Increase the output bus level control by +2 dB—for example, if it had read -5.0 dB, change it to -3.0 dB.
5. Play the song through once more to verify that clipping doesn't occur in the output bus.

Now that you have the highest possible level, go ahead and render to disk.

FREE MP3 EXPORTING

Sonar can save audio in MP3 format, but only if you pay to unlock the trial version MP3 encoder that expires after 30 days. This is because it's necessary to pay a license fee to use the Fraunhofer MP3 encoder, and Cakewalk doesn't absorb that cost—after all, not everyone wants or needs MP3 export capability.

However, there is a free alternative available at **http://cwenc.sourceforge.net**. Cwenc (Cakewalk Encoder), written and copyrighted by Mikkel Elmholdt, encodes to both MP3 and Ogg Vorbis file formats. Using it is simple: Download the program, run SETUP.EXE, and cwenc overwrites the existing Cakewalk MP3 encoder (mp3enc.exe) located in the Shared Files folder.

The web site includes detailed instructions on how to use the program to encode MP3 files, so we won't go over that material here. The short form version is after you go *File > Export > Audio,* select the *MP3* option (leave Format as "Export to Stereo File[s]" and Bit Depth as "16"). Click on "Export," and Sonar mixes the file to a temporary WAV file.

At this point the cwenc screen appears, where you can make various adjustments to the MP3 format, including bit rate, mono or stereo, and whether to create secondary files. Note that if you want to, you can also specify a particular input file other than what's being mixed down with Sonar, as well as its destination, thus allowing the program to serve as a stand-alone MP3 encoder.

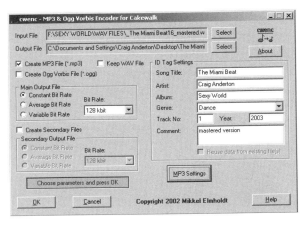

cwenc may be free, but it offers a lot of useful parameters for those who want to get their music out in MP3 format. You can also just go with the defaults if you're not sure what will work best.

Although the web site states cwenc has been tested with Windows 2000 and Cakewalk Home Studio, I can attest to the fact that it works just fine using Sonar 2 or 3 in conjunction with Windows XP. So if you need to encode to MP3 and would rather spend your money on, say, a good bottle of wine, then at least raise a toast to Mr. Elmholdt.

EXPORTING WAV FILES AND GROOVE CLIPS BY DRAG AND DROP

If you drag a Clip off the project and onto the desktop or a folder (open or closed), the Clip will remain at its origin, but will also be renamed and saved at the destination. A "Copying WAV File" bar graph indicator keeps track of the copy progress. You can even select multiple Clips, and drag them simultaneously to a destination folder.

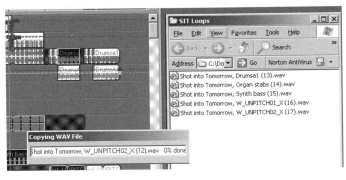

Several Clips have been selected, and dragged off to a folder for backup. The "Copying WAV File" progress indicator shows the copy progress for each Clip that's dragged over. In this case, five Clips have been saved. Note that this procedure saves the raw files, without the effects of any automation or plug-ins.

The file is renamed with the following useful format: [name of project], [name of Clip], and an ID number. This lets you see at a glance the project to which a file belongs. If you didn't name the Clip, the Clip name will simply say "Record" followed by a number.

However, there is a caution. When you go to Sonar to select the Clip(s) to drag-copy, the focus shifts away from the destination folder. Therefore, if you open up the folder then drag files over to it, after the copy process is complete you may not see the file names show up. So, click anywhere in the destination folder or its title bar to return focus to it after copying, or keep the mouse button held down at the destination until the copy procedure is complete. When you release the mouse button, focus will shift to the destination folder, and you'll see the files with their new names.

If you drag the files to a closed folder, then simply opening it should be enough to refresh the view. By the way, if you drag a Groove Clip (not just a WAV file) off to a folder for saving, it retains all its grooviness. But be aware that if you bring a non-Groove Clip file into Sonar, convert it to a Groove Clip, and then try to save it over the original file, the Groove Clip parameters will not be saved so "Save As" under a different name. This is a safety measure to prevent you from overwriting source files.

Also note that MP3 files can be Acidized in the Loop Construction window, but if you try to save them externally to the program, they will be converted to WAV format.

12

TROUBLESHOOTING AND OPTIMIZING

SONAR ANTI-FREEZE

I started having a weird problem with Sonar: It would work perfectly but upon exiting, would freeze up. If I hit "Ctrl-Alt-Del," a box would come up saying that Sonar was not responding. Selecting Sonar from the list of programs, then clicking on "End Task," would return the computer to normal operation. It had me baffled, so I contacted Sonar tech support, who had the answer.

When Sonar exits, it releases control over any drivers it's using, so the main reason for a freeze would be a lack of communication with a device's drivers. Normally, you can just deselect all the MIDI I/O from *Options > MIDI Devices,* deselect all audio devices found at *Options > Audio > Drivers,* and restart Sonar. You enable each driver one at a time, and exit after each enable—if the computer freezes, you've found out which driver is causing the problem.

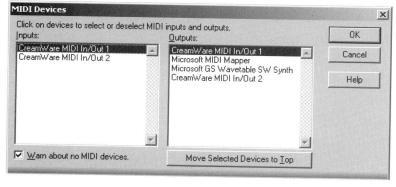

Look over the drivers Sonar is using by going Options > MIDI Devices and Options > Audio > Drivers. *Make sure there aren't any unneeded or obsolete MIDI or audio drivers, as Sonar will pout if it can't find a way to communicate with them.*

However, merely deselecting a MIDI driver from MIDI Devices still caused my computer to freeze, so stronger measures were required. At least it now seemed very likely that a MIDI driver was the problem. Support suggested the following, which worked for me:

1. With Sonar closed, delete the TTSSEQ.INI file from your system (normally found in the Sonar program folder).
2. Open Sonar; it will prompt you to select MIDI devices. Don't choose any and continue.
3. Close Sonar and see if it freezes. If it doesn't, then the problem is indeed MIDI driver-related.
4. Open Sonar, and select drivers one by one until you find the one that breaks the system.

In my case, it was one labelled "Generator Synthesizer," which was a holdover from a product I had reviewed on the same computer. I disabled it, and all was well. The same kind of fix applies to rogue audio drivers. The moral of the story: Don't always trust uninstall routines!

MYSTERIES OF THE AUD.INI FILE

The AUD.INI file is a configuration file located within the Sonar program folder on your C: drive that you can edit using a text editor like Windows Notepad. Although there are a lot of parameters you should probably leave as is, several of them can be modified to customize the Sonar experience.

Note that unlike the registry, if all else fails, you can just delete the file. The next time you start Sonar, it will build a new one. In fact, some people recommend doing this every now and then to purge such things as old entries from former sound cards. In any event, here are some tweaks.

Bigger Graphics Cache

On a recent long tune, as I worked more with the song, the time required to move or edit digital audio Clips started to lengthen. Just dragging a copy of a Clip a measure or two, or scrolling from one end of the file to the other, slowed down as I added more and more Clips.

Cakewalk support said this is particularly likely to occur if you use lots of Groove Clips in a tune (which I was). The fix is to increase the Picture Cache from the default of 20 MB. Go to the Sonar folder and open the AUD.INI file in Notepad. In the [Aud] section, locate the "PicCacheMB" parameter. Change 20 to 200, save the file, then restart. It should make a difference.

• Troubleshooting and Optimizing •

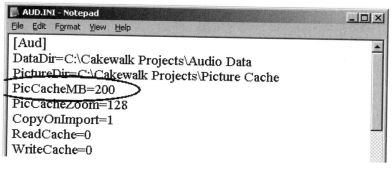

The AUD.INI file has a bunch of tweakable parameters. The "PicCacheMB" parameter in the [Aud] section (circled for clarity), can be increased to speed up graphics when using lots of Groove Clips.

WHERE TO CACHE YOUR DATA STASH

Speaking of the picture cache, when you install Sonar, this defaults to the path C:\Cakewalk Projects\Picture Cache. But think about your C drive: it holds your operating system, as well as program files. Cakewalk defaults to putting audio data inside the same Cakewalk Projects file on your C drive, so you're pulling a lot of data off that poor, overworked drive. Granted, modern hard drives are fast, so you may not notice any problems. But if you have a lot of hard disk tracks with numerous loops that require significant graphics redraws, consider storing your audio and graphics data elsewhere.

To do this, go *Options > Global* and select the "Audio Data" tab. This shows the path for the "Global Audio" and "Picture" folders. Simply create new folders for this data on the desired drives, and enter the new path in the appropriate fields.

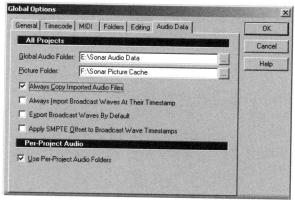

The "Global Options" area has a lot of ways to customize Sonar; under the "Audio Data" tab, you can set up paths for the global audio folder and picture folder. Note that the "Folders" tab lets you specify other locations, such as the default locations where Sonar should look for video files, drum maps, templates, etc.

For example, I have a fast E drive that's dedicated to storing data, which is where the Cakewalk Audio resides. The picture data lives on drive F. As a result of separating out the data, when doing hard disk recording, the hard disk tracks are pulled off disk at the fastest possible speed from a dedicated (and of course, defragmented!) drive.

For the most trouble-free transition when changing to a new file path, I suggest copying over (not moving) the existing folders to their new destinations before opening Sonar. Then open Sonar, change the file paths as described above, and close Sonar. Open it again, and now your projects will reference the new folder locations. If everything works as it's supposed to, you may then erase the original audio and picture folders.

THE CAKEWALK.INI FILE: AUDIO WIDGET CUSTOMIZATION

The parameters within a track—volume, pan, trim, FX, auxes, in, outs, etc.—can be changed from the standard layout. This is important because as Sonarians know, resizing the track can show greater or fewer parameters. Ideally, you want the parameters you use the most toward the top, so you can keep a small track "window" yet see the parameters you need.

For example, in the default Tracks Pane, the Vol—Pan—Trim "trinity" are followed by the In and Out connections, then various other parameters. I always wanted a way to move the In and Out parameters to the bottom, as once adjusted I don't really need to deal with them any further. However the FX field was something I *did* want toward the top, at least when using a horizontal rather than vertical field. And ideally, the Out would be on the same line as the Phase and Interleave, while In—my least adjusted parameter—would languish on the bottom.

The secret to rearranging these audio widgets this lies within the CAKE-WALK.INI file, found within the Sonar folder (typically the path is *C: drive > Program Files > Cakewalk > Sonar*). This can be edited with a text editor like Notepad. Add the following anywhere within the file:

[Audio Widgets]
W0=Volume
W1=Pan
W2=Trim
W3=Input

W4=Output
W5=FX
W6=Aux
W7=Phase
W8=Interleave

This is the default order. To change the order, simply re-number and re-arrange the lines. Here's what I use:

[Audio Widgets]
W0=Volume
W1=Pan
W2=Trim
W3=FX
W4=Aux
W5=Output
W6=Phase
W7=Interleave
W8=Input

The names are not case-sensitive, but if any "keys" are missing or otherwise incorrect, Sonar will revert to the defaults.

MIDI tracks can be similarly modified; here are the default widget parameters (which I didn't change):

[MIDI Widgets]
W0=Volume
W1=Pan
W2=Trim
W3=Input
W4=Output
W5=Channel
W6=Bank
W7=Patch
W8=Key
W9=Time
W10=FX
W11=Chorus
W12=Reverb

Incidentally, you can edit the CAKEWALK.INI file in the middle of a project, and these edits affect any subsequent tracks you add. But this is of limited use because next time you load the project, all tracks will simply grab the current CAKEWALK.INI settings anyway.

FILE NAMING ISSUES

Sonar won't save a file name with illegal DOS characters, and will give an error message if you try. This is particularly mysterious to people who have moved to Sonar from the Mac, as the Mac will let you use just about any character in a file name.

However, also be aware that if the file name ends with a question mark, Sonar will simply refuse to save the file, and not tell you why.

RESTARTING YOUR ENGINES

When you push Sonar hard, like doing complex playback and editing at the same time, sometimes the audio engine gets distracted. If you don't hear any audio, make sure the Audio Engine is enabled. To do this, click on the button just to the left of the "Reset" button (the one with the exclamation mark) in the Transport.

The reset button performs a similar function for MIDI data. It clears all stuck notes and immediately silences any MIDI notes that are currently sounding. You can also access this by going *Transport > Reset.*

The audio engine enable and reset buttons can come in handy should Sonar stall.

If you need to hit these buttons a lot, then look into your system for possible problems. Excessive audio dropouts could be due to driver problems, or trying to set too low a latency.

MIDI RECORDING PROBLEMS

Some Sonar users have a problem recording real time MIDI information from a controller keyboard, even though notes play when keys are pressed, and there's clear indication that MIDI data is being received. Here are some suggestions.

First, check the keyboard button that appears in the System Tray when you open Sonar. Playing your MIDI keyboard should illuminate the input "LED" (even if all MIDI options in the program are disabled). If the input doesn't light, check your interface, interface driver, cables, and keyboard—the problem is not within Sonar.

If all seems well, then there are probably some misset preferences. Here's how to set them up; you only need do this once, unless you want to make subsequent changes.

Under *Options > MIDI devices,* verify that the desired MIDI input and output ports are highlighted and at the top of the list. If a different MIDI port is on top (like Microsoft MIDI Mapper), highlight the desired device and click on "Move Selected Devices to Top." Also, check the "Warn about no MIDI devices" box. If some problem doesn't allow Sonar to recognize the MIDI ports, you'll be notified when you load the program.

Still not happening? Go *Options > Global >* "MIDI" tab. Under "Record," make sure that "Notes" is checked. I also recommend checking at least "Controller," "Patch Changes," and "Pitch Wheel." Enable "Key/Channel Aftertouch" prior to recording parts when you want to record this data, then disable afterward to avoid recording superfluous data. I usually leave "System Exclusive" unchecked unless I plan to do some dumps into the program.

Now that the preferences are set, select a MIDI track by clicking on the track number, then click on the track's "R" button to arm recording. Finally, click on the Transport "Record" button, and notes should appear in the selected track (Clips Pane) as you play them.

IMPROVE MIDI TIMING WITH SLOWER COMPUTERS

When doing MIDI, do you really need 960 PPQ? You can improve MIDI timing accuracy on slower computers by going *Options > Project > Clock,* and selecting a lower PPQ value (*e.g.,* 240 or 360). I doubt that even most golden-ears types will notice any substantial difference between higher and lower resolution settings.

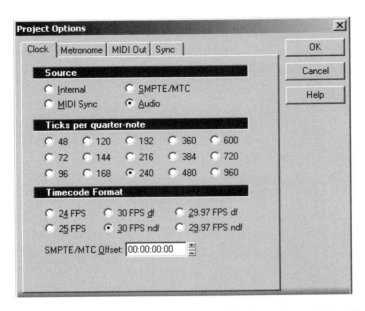

You can modify the MIDI resolution under "Project Options." The lower the resolution, the tighter the timing with slower computers.

SAFE MODE

If you try to open a Sonar project that uses a plug-in currently missing from your system, or if your project has become corrupted, try opening the project in "safe mode." This loads plug-ins one by one, and gives you the option to reject loading ones that either don't work or aren't present on your system.

To do this from the *File > Open* menu, after selecting the file name, hold down the Shift key and click on "Open." If you're selecting the file from the "Most Recently Used Files" list in the File menu or the "Open a Recent Project" drop-down menu from the Quick Start window, click on the file name while holding down the Shift key. This will open up the "Safe Mode" dialog box where you can either load a plug-in, load all plug-ins, reject a plug-in, or reject all plug-ins.

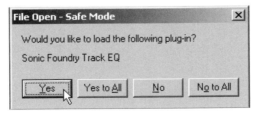

Sonar gives you the opportunity to load plug-ins one at a time to find out if one of them is causing a problem when you try to open a file.

• *Troubleshooting and Optimizing* •

SOLVING THE HALION PRESET PROBLEM

HALion is a popular virtual sampler made by Steinberg. Although VSampler3, included with Sonar, can load HALion presets, there may still be times when you want to use the HALion program itself (particularly HALion 2, which includes some wonderful filters).

However, some Sonar users have said they can't get HALion to load any presets (and have reported having this problem with other VST instruments as well). You can, but you have to know where to look in HALion to do the loading.

Note that even when running HALion under VST, you're cautioned against using the standard VST open program options, and instead to use the small File box located within HALion. Unfortunately, that doesn't show up under VST Adapter, but no worries.

1. Go to HALion's Options page.
2. Under Import Options, select "Import Audio Files."
3. Specify the desired type of HALion file (.fxp, .fxb, or all)
4. Choose the file from the dialog box, and click "Open."

As you can't bring in files using HALion's file box when running it under VST Adapter, use the HALion Option menu's "Import" feature to call up a preset instead.

13

BONUS TIPS

Looking for a few extra goodies? Here are some short but sweet tips.

- The Snap to Grid function in each view is independent. For example, the Track View can have different snap parameters compared to the Piano Roll view.

- You can lock editing operations to envelopes only in the Clips Pane. Do this by clicking on the "Envelope Tool" button in the Track Pane (or just type "E"). To return to the normal editing mode, click on the "Select" button or type "T."

- One of my favorite keyboard equivalents is "N," which turns snap-to-grid on or off in the main Track View and the MIDI views.

- To quickly hide tracks, select them in the Tracks Pane (or select Clips in the Clips view that belong to tracks you want to hide), then type "Shift-H."

- To show all tracks instantly, type "A" while in any view.

- Type "I" while in any view to toggle between showing and hiding the Inspector.

- Note that the Inspector can have a wide or narrow view. Right-click on an empty space in the Inspector, and either check or uncheck "Narrow Strip."

- When editing a drum map, to assign all identical channels and output ports to a different channel or output port, press "Ctrl+Shift" while changing *any* channel or port.

- To change a note's properties in the Staff or Piano Roll view, right-click on the note.

- When configuring a generic control surface in Sonar, use the "Alt+L" keyboard equivalent to go into Learn mode.

- Go *Edit > History* to access recent undoable edits you've made.

- If you have a scrolling mouse and the pointer is over the Track or Clips view, the mouse wheel performs the same function as the Track View's vertical scroll bar.

- To solo or unsolo any selected track or group of tracks, type the "/" key on your QWERTY keyboard.

- You can insert an audio track by right-clicking on the Track Pane and selecting "Insert Audio Track." But if you're in a hurry, click on an existing track of the type you want (MIDI or audio), then hit the "Insert" key on your QWERTY keyboard. Done!

- Sonar can overlay a grid line at measure boundaries. Right-click on a space in the Clips Pane, choose "View-Options," then select "Display Vertical Rules."

- In any field where entering a number specifies a value, there are four ways to vary numerical values after clicking on a field: Type in the value, use the "spinner" control toward to the right of the numerical, use the numeric keypad's (+) or (-) keys to increment/decrement respectively, or use the [ ] keys to increment/decrement by larger values (*e.g.,* by tens in the tempo display).

- To preview a selected loop in the Loop Construction window, hit "Shift+Spacebar." You can also use this to stop the preview if it's already playing.

- To return to the beginning of a tune at any time, type "W" ("reWind").

• Bonus Tips •

- To return to the beginning of a tune and immediately begin playback, type "Shift-W."

- If you have several projects open simultaneously, for example to drag and drop files among them, you can often make this go more easily with the *Window > Tile in Rows or Window > Tile* in Columns options.

- For a reference list of keyboard shortcuts, go *Help > Keyboard Shortcuts* and click on the "Print" button.

- To split an entire arrangement of Clips, for example to cut or paste a verse, select all tracks ("Ctrl-A"), place the now time at the desired split point, and type "S."

- You don't have to click the Lasso Zoom button to zoom in on a selection; just select with the standard lasso while holding down the "Z" key. When you release the mouse, the window will zoom in on the selected area.

- Press "Ctrl-Tab" to navigate through the various open Sonar views.

- Double-clicking on most controls will reset them to their default positions.

- If you've slip-edited a Clip and want to discard the excess, right-click on the Clip and select "Apply Trimming."

- To scrub multiple audio tracks, select the Scrub tool, hold the left mouse button, and drag across the Time Ruler.

- In the status line at the bottom of the screen, there are three boxes to the left of the available Disk Space indicator. These show if any mute, solo, or arm record buttons are selected. They also serve as master "off" buttons for these functions—for example, if a slot says "SOLO," clicking on it turns off all solo buttons.

- Bundle files (.cwb suffix) are limited to 2 GB due to limitations in the Windows operating system. To back up a project with more than 2 GB of data, place all audio data in a per-project audio folder and back that up.

- Networked with a Mac? Although Sonar can import AIFF files, you can also just drag them into the Clips Pane.

- To scrub multiple audio tracks, select the Scrub tool, hold the left mouse button, and drag across the Time Ruler.

- Don't forget that scrubbed sounds appear at the sound card outputs— sample the more interesting noises!

- Drawing a "marquee" around Clips selects the entire Clip. To select just a portion of a Clip, hold the "Alt" key while click-dragging.

- In the Synth Rack view, you can step through the synth patches using the (-) and (=) keys to decrement and increment patch numbers, respectively.

- Will you need to pay for a Sonar upgrade? Generally, versions where numbers change to the right of the decimal point are free upgrades; if numbers change to the left of the decimal point, it's a paid upgrade.

- To change the Draw tool in the Piano Roll view to an Erase tool, just hold down "Alt." Memorize this—it will save you time!

- Go *Transport > Record Options* to determine whether material being recorded to an existing track will replace old data or blend with it.

- To choose whether the space bar does start/stop or start/pause for playback, go *Options > Global* and respectively check or uncheck "On Stop, Rewind to Now Marker."

- To insert a time signature change, go *Insert > Meter/Key Change*.

- To revert to a previous zoom level in the Clips Pane or Piano Roll view, press the "U" key.

- You can drag-and-drop Sonar Clips into several digital audio editing programs, such as Wavelab and Cool Edit Pro 2. Unfortunately, the reverse is not true.

- To remove a track's contents but leave all track properties intact, use the *Track > Wipe* command. Unlike "Cut," the track data is not placed on the clipboard.

- To record on multiple tracks simultaneously, just arm each track to be recorded, and make sure they all have the correct input assignment.

- All "View" key commands consist of Alt + a number. For example, "Alt+1" is Loop Explorer, "Alt+3" is Console View, and "Alt+5" is Piano Roll view.

- To close the top window, hit "Ctrl-F4."

ABOUT THE AUTHOR

CRAIG ANDERTON got an early start in the world of music: By his 22nd birthday he had recorded three albums, toured most of the USA east of the Mississippi, and played Carnegie Hall.

He began his recording career as a teen-ager in 1967 with the Philadelphia-based group "Mandrake Memorial" and was one of the first musicians to use synthesizers on stage, having built his first synth in 1968. He also invented a semi-programmable, all-electronic drum machine in 1970.

During the early 70s he played sessions on both guitar and synthesizer for Epic, Metromedia, Columbia, RCA, United Artists, and other labels; he has also produced three albums by classical guitarist Linda Cohen, was mixdown/production consultant on Valley in the Clouds by David Arkenstone, and mixed several cuts on Emerald (by Brewer, Tingstad, and Rumbel, recently re-released). More recently, he has found success in the European dance music scene, with cuts on several compilation CDs. Rolling Stone reviewed his solo CD Forward Motion, a "desktop CD" written, recorded, and mixed in his home studio, and called it "one of those rare instrumental electronic albums that is not mere New Age tapioca."

During the mid-70s Craig started writing for publications including Guitar Player, Keyboard, Rolling Stone, and Mix. He has also been published in major British, German, French, Belgian, Japanese, Dutch, Polish, Spanish, Swiss, and Italian publications. He coined the term "electronic musician" and in 1985, was the driving force behind transforming Polyphony magazine into Electronic Musician magazine, which he edited for its first five years. Currently he is a regular contributor to EQ, Keyboard, Pro Sound News, Performing Songwriter, Sound on Sound (UK), and Keyboards—Recording and Computers (Germany).

Throughout his career, Craig has also been extremely active as a lecturer. He has given seminars on many aspects of musical electronics at colleges, music stores, and conventions in 37 states and 10 countries (and in three different languages). He has also designed sounds for Alesis, Digitech, Discrete Drums, E-mu, Ensoniq, Northstar, Optical Media, M-Audio, Native Instruments, Peavey, Prosonus, Steinberg, Wizoo, and Yamaha. His most recent sample CDs are "Technoid Guitars" (Steinberg), "Turbulent Filth Monsters" (Discrete Drums), and "AdrenaLinn Guitars" (M-Audio).

In 1998 he started playing on a semi-regular basis with Rei$$dorf Force, a German experimental electronic music band headquartered in Cologne, and performing solo under his own name. He also appears occasionally as a guest artist with the group Air Liquide. Several of his tunes have been remixed for the European market.